BOOK 3

The Central Auditory Processing Kit™

Mary Ann Mokhemar

Skill Area: Central Auditory Processing
Ages: 6 through 14
Grades: 1 through 9

LinguiSystems, Inc.
3100 4th Avenue
East Moline, IL 61244-9700

800-776-4332

FAX: 800-577-4555
E-mail: service@linguisystems.com
Web: linguisystems.com

Printed in the U.S.A.
ISBN 10: 0-7606-0306-5
ISBN 13: 978-0-7606-0306-2

About the Author

Mary Ann Mokhemar, MS, CCC-SLP, earned master's degrees in both speech pathology and audiology from the University of Michigan in 1973. Later, she received an Ed.S. from the University of Georgia, with a major emphasis in speech pathology and reading disability. Mary Ann's intense interest in central auditory processing issues began ten years ago and continues today. She has provided remediation services in public and private schools, hospitals, and rehabilitation centers. She has also supervised student clinicians at a university clinic, and she maintains a private practice in addition to working in the public schools in Buford, Georgia.

In her spare time, Mary Ann enjoys running and biking to prepare for Atlanta's annual 6K Peachtree Road Race, run each July 4th. She also drives her husband crazy by constantly revising recipes he loves, in a never-ending effort to create something even better!

The Central Auditory Processing Kit is Mary Ann's first publication with LinguiSystems.

Dedication . . . .

To my daughter, Miriam — Life has never been so good.

To my parents, my uncle, and my husband — Thank you for always expecting the best from me.

Table of Contents

The Index for each unit is listed
at the beginning of the unit.

Book 1   Auditory Memory

Book 2   Auditory Discrimination

              Auditory Closure

              Auditory Synthesis

Processing. Language Processing. Auditory Processing. These words and phrases seem to dominate what we hear and read, from parent magazines to professional catalog offerings to child-study team discussions. The speech-language pathologist often plays a critical role in gathering relevant information and evaluating it to present a clear, accurate picture of a student with central auditory processing deficits (CAPD). The professional gathers information from across the environments of home and school and then carefully analyzes the information to prepare a prescriptive response. The following list specifies what the speech-language pathologist needs to consider and accomplish in conducting such an evaluation:

Understand and describe the student's behaviors, both at home and at school.

Understand relevant speech, language, and listening skill areas and how they affect academic performance and everyday interactions.

Know which formal tests to use to delineate areas of weakness within speech and language functioning.

Understand the tests used in audiological testing and their implications in preparing the prescriptive response.

Understand the role of the medical doctor in attempting to rule out attention deficit hyperactivity or hypoactivity disorders.

Understand the role of the learning disability specialist and the tests used in attempting to rule out a learning disability.

Examine language arts-related performances within the student's classroom or classrooms, including observations of behaviors, grades on report cards and projects, test scores for formalized tests such as *Cogats* and *ITBS*, and patterns of errors.

Certain behaviors are often associated with children presenting with CAPD. These behaviors are listed in the box on page 6. Please note that these behaviors can also be found in children with learning disabilities and/or attention deficit hyperactivity disorder. As with most disorders, not every child with CAPD exhibits all of these behaviors, and the intensity of a given child's behaviors may vary across time and situations.

The auditory skill areas most commonly addressed in intervention for children with CAPD are listed and described on pages 7-8. The corresponding units of the three books in this program provide specific training exercises to improve each of these skill areas.

Characteristics of Children with CAPD

Overall performance for auditory functioning is poor

- Responds inconsistently to auditory stimuli
- Difficulty localizing sound sources
- Easily distracted; short attention span
- Unusually bothered by loud or sudden noises or noisy environments
- Appears to perform better in quieter settings
- Poor auditory memory skills for numbers and words
- Poor sequencing skills and sense of rhythm

Weaknesses in receptive and expressive language

- Misunderstands what is said; confuses similar-sounding words
- Requires information to be repeated several times; often asks *Huh?* or *What?*
- Finds abstract information difficult to understand when presented orally
- Difficulty following simple and complex oral directions
    - Confuses or forgets directions when several are given at one time
    - Has difficulty with delayed directions
- Hesitant speech; responds to questions and instructions slowly or with delay
- Weak vocabulary
- Difficulty singing in tune
- Difficulty with spelling, reading, and writing
    - Difficulty with phonics and speech sound discrimination
    - Confusion with, or reversal of, letters
    - Poor reading comprehension

Often viewed as a behavior problem

- Fidgety behaviors; hyperactivity; often irritable
- Often disorganized and forgetful; tendency to procrastinate
- Unusually tired at the end of the day
- Mixed dominance; confusion between left and right
- Low self-esteem; tendency to be depressed and feel overburdened
- Often viewed as immature; easily frustrated
- Not motivated, or negative, about school
- Pragmatically inappropriate due to difficulty following conversations

Auditory memory involves immediate and delayed recall of numbers, words, sentences, and directions. Just because a person can repeat well does not mean that he can remember well! Effective auditory memory involves interpretation. Weaknesses in this area may translate into academic difficulties as follows:

> Difficulty recalling letters, words, and numbers
>
> Inconsistent recall for addresses and phone numbers
>
> Forgetfulness with sound-symbol relationships
>
> Difficulty following all parts of oral directions

Auditory discrimination involves differentiating isolated sounds in words and words in sentences. At a very basic level, auditory discrimination may involve discrimination of nonlinguistic material such as environmental, animal, and musical sounds. Weaknesses in this area may translate into academic difficulties as follows:

> Difficulty understanding oral directions
>
> Difficulty learning letter sounds and letter names
>
> Poor spelling, reading, and writing skills
>
> Tendency to repeat words, numbers, and directions incorrectly

Auditory closure involves the ability to supply information that was not heard completely. The ability to predict this information is based upon a student's ability to use the context of information effectively. Weaknesses in this area may translate into academic difficulties as follows:

> Difficulty understanding speech in noise
>
> Poor vocabulary
>
> Poor syntax
>
> Difficulty with sound recognition and sound blending in phonics tasks

Auditory synthesis involves the abilities to form a word from individual sounds and to identify individual sounds in words as they occur within words or sentences. Weaknesses in this area may translate into academic difficulties as follows:

> Difficulty with phonics
>
> Difficulty with grammar
>
> Difficulty interpreting word stress

Auditory figure-ground involves listening in the presence of background noise from sources such as air conditioning units, noisy classrooms, radios, TVs, cafeterias, and playgrounds. Weaknesses in this area may translate into the following academic difficulties, listed on page 8.

Distractibility	Easily frustrated
Inattention	Negative feelings about school
Fidgety behavior	Procrastination
Intolerance and irritability	

Auditory cohesion involves higher-level linguistic processing skills, such as the ability to follow complicated conversations, understand jokes and riddles, make inferences, and draw conclusions. Weaknesses in this area may translate into academic difficulties as follows:

Poor note-taking skills

Poor reading comprehension, particularly compared to reading decoding strategies

Pragmatically inappropriate behaviors

Difficulty with written expression

Auditory binaural integration (interhemispheric functioning) involves the ability to make transfers between verbal and motor activities. Weaknesses in this area may translate into academic difficulties as follows:

Difficulty functioning in classroom centers

Difficulty learning within a whole-language environment

Difficulty taking notes and writing to dictation

Difficulty with music-related skills

Assessment and Diagnosis of CAPD . . . .

Speech-language pathologists often use the following instruments, arranged by publisher, to assess CAPD:

American Guidance Systems

Goldman-Fristoe Woodcock Test of Auditory Discrimination

Kaufman Test of Educational Achievement (KTEA)—particularly the Reading Decoding and Reading Comprehension subtests

Oral and Written Language Scales (OWLS)—particularly the Listening Comprehension Scale

LinguiSystems, Inc.

Language Processing Test-Revised (LPT-R)

The Listening Test

The Phonological Awareness Test

*The Test of Problem Solving, Elementary-*Revised *(TOPS-R)*

Western Psychological Services

Wepman's Auditory Discrimination Test (ADT)

Wepman's Auditory Memory Battery

Precision Acoustics

Auditory Continuous Performance Test (ACPT)

The Psychological Corporation

Clinical Evaluation of Language Fundamentals-3 (CELF-3)—particularly the Concepts and Directions, Recalling Sentences, and Word Classes subtests

Wechsler Individual Achievement Tests (WIAT)—particularly the Reading Decoding and Reading Comprehension, Oral Expression, Written Expression, and Listening Comprehension subtests

PRO-ED

Detroit Tests of Learning Aptitude-4 (DTLA-4)—particularly the Sentence Imitation, Reverse Letters, Word Sequences, and Story Sequences subtests

Lindamood Auditory Conceptualization Test (LAC)

Test of Language Development-Primary (TOLD-P:3)—particularly the Sentence Imitation, Word Discrimination, and Phonemic Analysis subtests

Token Test for Children and *Revised Token Test (RTT)*

Test of Auditory Perceptual Skills-Revised (TAPS-R)

The following audiological diagnostic instruments are often used for CAPD testing:

A Screening Test for Auditory Processing Disorders (SCAN)—This screening instrument consists of three subtests as follows:

1. Filtered Words—assesses auditory closure; may reflect difficulties in comprehending words within the acoustic environment and filling in auditory information that is lost to background noise

2. Auditory Figure-Ground—assesses word discrimination abilities in the presence of background noise; may reflect difficulties in focusing on auditory information within the typical noisy environment

3. Competing Words—assesses binaural integration via a dichotic speech task; may reflect difficulties with the ability to store and recall speech information

A Screening Test for Auditory Processing Disorders in Adolescents and Adults (SCAN-A)—This screening instrument differs from the *SCAN* in that there are a greater number of words, less delay in presentation, and an additional subtest for competing sentences; this subtest may reflect difficulties with binaural separation.

Phonemic Synthesis Test—assesses sound blending, discrimination skills, articulation, processing time, and sequencing; may reflect difficulties with auditory closure and decoding activities

Staggered Spondaic Word Test (SSW)—assesses binaural integration within a linguistically-loaded format; may reflect difficulties with decoding or receptive language weaknesses

Dichotic Digits Test (DDT)—assesses binaural integration within a non-linguistically-loaded format; may reflect difficulties with binaural separation in noise

Pitch Pattern Sequence Test (PPS)—assesses temporal patterning; may reflect difficulties with understanding inflectional patterns and recognizing and using prosodic speech features

Duration Pattern Sequence Test (DPS)—assesses temporal patterning; may reflect difficulties with the prosodic speech features

The sample case study below illustrates a typical report from an assessment of a child referred for suspected auditory deficits.

Sample Case Study . . . .

This ten-year-old, fifth-grade student was seen to rule out a central auditory processing weakness. Relevant medical history includes frequent middle ear infections in early childhood. Behaviors observed by the mother reflect that the student often needs messages repeated; has difficulty spelling dictated words; has problems following oral directions that require remembering a sequence of commands; shows confusion with the order of syllables; shows difficulty with the phonetic spelling approach; exhibits extreme distractibility in a noisy situation; has poor retention of verbal information after a short period of time; and misinterprets words, phrases, and sentences.

Audiological Evaluation

Pure-tone testing revealed normal hearing sensitivity with a slight asymmetry in the low frequencies, the left ear being the poorer ear.

Speech recognition ability (stimuli presented dichotically at +5 s/n) was 84% for the right ear and 96% for the left ear at 45 dBHL. This is within normal limits.

Tympanometry revealed normal Type "A" tracings bilaterally. A visual inspection of the ears was normal.

Distortion Product Otoacoustic Emission (OAE) testing revealed slightly reduced emissions for the left ear at 1000 and 1500 Hz. Emissions were present in the normal range for all frequencies in the right ear.

Central Tests

A *Screening for Auditory Processing Disorders (SCAN)* test was given.

The Filtered Words subtest is a low-pass filtered speech test that assesses auditory closure, the ability to "fill in" the missing parts of speech. The student's score was very poor for this skill (1st percentile).

The Auditory Figure Ground (AFG) subtest assesses word discrimination abilities in the presence of competing background noise. The student's score was fair for this skill (9th percentile).

The Competing Sentences subtest is a dichotic speech task that reflects the development and maturation of the auditory system. The student's score was poor for this skill (2nd percentile). The pattern of errors in the left ear only suggests a possible delay in the maturation of the auditory system. Left ear performance usually does improve over time.

The Competing Words subtest is a dichotic test in which different speech stimuli are presented to the two ears simultaneously. The student's score was fair for this skill (2nd percentile). A depressed score may suggest that a child's auditory system is functioning similar to that of a younger child.

The *Staggered Spondaic Word (SSW)* test assesses binaural integration and requires the subject to respond to spondee words presented to both ears. The second syllable of the first word and the first syllable of the second word are presented simultaneously. The patient is asked to repeat all four words. Scores were in the normal range for all four test conditions. The student did have a significant number of reversals. He could not remember the four words in sequence, so he would often repeat the second compound word first, followed by the initial compound word. This compensatory strategy is often displayed when a child has poor auditory memory or sequencing skills.

The *Phonemic Synthesis Test* involves blending sounds into words. It tests discrimination skills, articulation, blending, processing time, and sequencing. The test was given under earphones at 50 dBHL bilaterally. The student's score placed him at the early first grade level. The student had significant difficulty with voiceless blends. He seemed to show difficulty discriminating the phoneme sounds /s/ from /sh/ or /st/ and also /sh/ from /ch/.

The student's test results are consistent with an auditory decoding deficit, characterized by poor performance on tests of monaural, low-redundancy speech and speech-in-noise.

These children often exhibit difficulty in reading, particularly when an auditory phonics approach to reading is applied. Likewise, speech-to-print skills, vocabulary, syntax, and semantic skills may be weak. These students usually do well in math because phonemic decoding is not required. Since this deficit reduces a child's phonemic representation ability, sound blending, discrimination, and retention of phonemes is poor. The deficit manifests itself in the inability to achieve auditory closure due to breakdown in the intrinsic redundancy of the central auditory nervous system when portions of the auditory signal are distorted or missing. Although the student showed no significant weakness with auditory memory skills, auditory sequencing problems were evident throughout testing.

Recommendations

Repetition may help children with closure deficits, but only if the repetition is acoustically clearer than the original presentation of the message. The child's ability to comprehend the message will be good as long as the child is able to decode the message. Improving the acoustic clarity of the signal may be achieved by preferential seating away from noise sources in the classroom and using an assistive listening device during therapy sessions to improve the signal-to-noise ratio. Implement activities to develop and strengthen auditory sequencing skills.

The student may benefit most from phoneme training at the syllable level, specific training of speech-to-print skills, auditory closure activities designed to teach the use of contextual clues, and auditory sequencing of speech sounds and patterns of loudness and rhythm. These activities should be conducted by a speech pathologist.

An analysis of this report indicates therapy direction as follows:

Auditory closure activities

Activities involving word discrimination in the presence of background noise

Auditory memory activities

Auditory sequencing activities

Sound blending activities

This chapter focuses on the ability to listen to relevant auditory stimuli despite the presence of distracting background stimuli of varying intensity levels. The chapter begins with building skills for following directions in noise and finishes with building skills for following lecture materials. The progression for background noise is as follows:

Progression for Background Noise

low-level, continuous	appliances, such as a fan, a clothes dryer, or a dishwasher
non-specific music	a radio or CD featuring music that the student finds very uninteresting/nondistracting; volume low, yet distinctive
specific music	a radio or CD featuring music that the student finds very appealing/distracting
radio talk shows	initially presented with low, yet distinctive, volume; later presented with varying volume levels to better mirror the varied volume levels found within most classrooms
television	The student sits with his/her back towards the TV; a program of no interest to the student is featured. Once the student masters this level, feature programs of great interest and use a remote control to vary volume levels.

Following Directions

The activities in this section reflect the above hierarchy as the student follows directions in a variety of listening environments. Each lesson includes both gross-motor and fine-motor directions. Materials needed for the gross-motor directions are listed for each lesson. For all fine-motor lessons, have the following materials available:

pencil   pen   box of crayons   box of markers

The information on the following page presents the ideal way to introduce competing background noise for each level of training in following directions.

Background Noise for Levels 1-5 of Following Directions

Level 1: Low-Level, Continuous Noise

Provide a background noise that is fairly constant in volume and intensity, such as the noise from an air conditioner, a fan, or a washing machine. An alternate source of this type of noise is highway traffic. You might want to pre-record this type of sound on a tape recorder so you can play the tape whenever necessary.

Level 2: Non-Specific Music

Provide a background noise of music that is not particularly interesting to the student. "Elevator music" works well here. You could also try classical music that isn't too dramatic or doesn't vary the volume a great deal. Keep the volume low enough to keep the music from distracting the student, yet loud enough to hear distinctly.

Level 3: Specific Music

Check with the student to find out what type(s) of music the student finds particularly interesting. If possible, let the student provide appropriate audio tapes or CDs. Otherwise, gather the appropriate music and play it during training sessions. Maintain the volume at a level that is not distracting, but is loud enough to hear distinctly.

Level 4: Radio Talk Shows

Radio talk shows add the element of connected speech as a background factor, but most of these shows won't be particularly enticing to the student. Also, choose talk shows that don't discuss controversial or provocative issues that might be too distracting.

Begin with a low volume. Increase the volume as the student shows ability to screen out this distraction. Continue increasing the volume until you match normal classroom volume. Also, vary the volume as the student gains proficiency to help the student practice adjusting to varying noise levels.

Level 5: Television

Begin with shows that are not especially interesting to the student. Gradually feature shows that are more appealing to the student. As with the radio talk shows, use a variety of volume levels once the student is fairly skilled in "tuning out" this interesting background noise.

Tell the student, "I'll give you some directions to follow. Pay attention to the directions, not the noise you hear in the background." Throughout these exercises, use low-level, continuous noise, such as a fan or a dishwasher.

Gross-Motor Response

Materials: pencil, telephone, paper

1. Stand on one foot.
2. Point to the door.
3. Walk to the door.
4. Touch your toes.
5. Raise your hand.
6. Hop back to your seat.
7. Name something that is blue.
8. Show me the pencil.
9. Point to the telephone.
10. Give a piece of paper to me.

Fine-Motor Response

Give the student a copy of page 17. Present the following directions.

Look at Row 1.

• Write the letter *A* to the right of the kite and the letter *Z* to the left of the star.

• Write the number *2* on the ice cream cone and draw a circle around the kite.

• Draw a line from the ice cream cone to the kite and add another scoop of ice cream to the cone.

Look at Row 2.

• Write the number *2* to the left of the letter *B* and draw a line under the letter *A*.

• Draw a vertical line through the letter *A* and a diagonal line through the letter *C*.

• Make a check mark above the letter *C* and a triangle around the letter *B*.

Look at Row 3.

• Write the number *2* on the bowl of the spoon and draw a line under the handle of the hammer.

• Draw a box around the flower's petals and make a check mark above the spoon.

• Draw a small piece of wood next to the hammer. Then, draw a nail sticking out of it.

Following Directions

Name _____

Listen carefully to the directions for each row.

Row 1

Row 2

B   C   A

Row 3

Gross-Motor Response

Materials: pictures, clock

1. Touch your chin.
2. Show me your teeth.
3. Close the door.
4. Show me a picture.
5. Rest your head on the table.
6. Run to the chair.
7. Show me your thumbs.
8. Show me your fingernails.
9. Sing the birthday song.
10. Count the numbers on the clock.

Fine-Motor Response

Give the student a copy of page 19. Present the following directions.

Look at Row 1.

- Draw a box around the flag on the boat and write an *X* on the doorknob.

- Draw a vertical line between the door and the ball and a horizontal line between the boat and the door.

- Write the number *2* on the ball and make a check mark on the window of the door.

Look at Row 2.

- Write the number *4* above the meat and draw a box around the carrot.

- Draw a line from the grapes to the carrot. Then, write an *X* on the carrot.

- Circle the grapes and draw a small triangle to the left of the grapes.

Look at Row 3.

- Shade in the area where the two circles overlap and draw a line under the large circle.

- Cross out the smaller circle and write the letter *T* to the right of that circle.

- Draw a vertical line between the overlapping circles and the smallest circle. Then, draw a horizontal line through the largest circle.

Following Directions

Name _____

Listen carefully to the directions for each row.

Row 1

 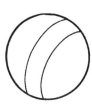

Row 2

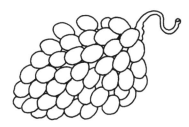  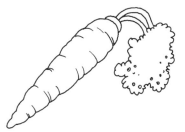

Row 3

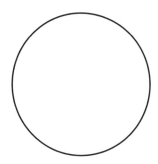 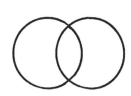

Gross-Motor Response

Materials: pencil, pencil sharpener, calendar, clock

1. Walk to the door.
2. Stick out your tongue.
3. Now, sit down.
4. Sharpen the pencil.
5. Tap your foot.
6. Show me the calendar.
7. Tell me the name of your best friend.
8. Wiggle your fingers.
9. Tell me your birthday.
10. Look at the clock.

Fine-Motor Response

Give the student a copy of page 21. Present the following directions.

Look at Row 1.

- Circle the triangle and draw a line under the ball.

- Draw a line from the triangle to the needle and write the number *4* between the ball and the needle.

- Draw a line over the needle and write an *X* on the ball.

Look at Row 2.

- Draw a circle around the flower and a frown face on the sun.

- Write the number *2* above the circles and shade in the area where the circles overlap.

- Write an X in the circle on the right and make a check mark in the circle on the left.

Look at Row 3.

- Draw a heart in the first square and an oval in the second square.

- Cross out the small square. Then, draw a diamond around it.

- Make a plus sign between the first two squares and an equal sign between the last two squares.

Following Directions

Listen carefully to the directions for each row.

Row 1

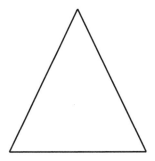 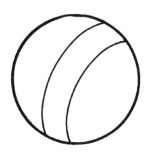 

Row 2

 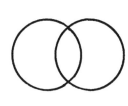 

Row 3

Gross-Motor Response

Materials: calendar, book

1. Sit down in the chair.
2. Close your mouth.
3. Tell me your name.
4. Look out the door.
5. Snap your fingers.
6. Tell me today's date.
7. Open the book.
8. Put your hands together.
9. Say "Ahh."
10. Cover your ears.

Fine-Motor Response

Give the student a copy of page 23. Present the following directions.

Look at Row 1.

- Circle the apple and write an *X* on one window of the house.

- Draw a knob on the door of the house and draw a line under the ball.

- Make a plus sign between the apple and the house and a minus sign between the house and the ball.

Look at Row 2.

- Circle the first number and draw a line under the *7*.

- Cross out the even number and make a plus sign above the number *3*.

- Write the number *4* next to the number *3* and a comma after the number *7*.

Look at Row 3.

- Write the letter *J* between the large and the medium balls and shade in the band on the medium ball.

- Draw a line from the large ball to the medium ball and draw a line under the small ball.

- Write a large number *2* above the large ball and also above the medium ball. Then, connect the numbers with a plus sign.

Following Directions

Name _____

Listen carefully to the directions for each row.

Row 1

  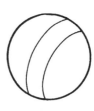

Row 2

8   3   7

Row 3

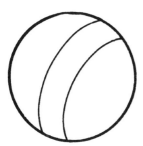 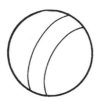

Gross-Motor Response

Materials: book, paper

1. Pick up the book.
2. Point to a word.
3. Give me a piece of paper.
4. Look at your sleeves.
5. Knock on the door.
6. Whisper your name.
7. Show me how you yawn.
8. Close the book.
9. Give the book to me.
10. Put your hands on the table.

Fine-Motor Response

Give the student a copy of page 25. Present the following directions.

Look at Row 1.

- Write the number *2* in the leaves of the tree and make a check mark above the cup.

- Draw a smiley face on the sun and a line under the tree.

- Draw a box around the cup and a small triangle above the tree.

Look at Row 3.

- Write the letter *E* in the square and draw a line under the heart.

- Draw a line above the plus sign. Then, circle the line.

- Make a plus sign in the square and another plus sign in the heart.

Look at Row 3.

- Draw a circle around the last letter and cross out the letter *M*.

- Draw a line under the vowel and draw a vertical line to the right of it.

- Draw a diamond around the *M* and connect the *E* and the *S* with a straight line.

Following Directions

Name _____

Listen carefully to the directions for each row.

Row 1

Row 2

Row 3

M   E   S

Gross-Motor Response

Materials: paper, wastebasket

1. Walk around the table.
2. Rip a piece of paper.
3. Open the door.
4. Close your eyes.
5. Open your eyes.
6. Stand up straight.
7. Show me how you stretch.
8. Put your ripped paper on the floor.
9. Now, throw the paper away.
10. Clap your hands.

Fine-Motor Response

Give the student a copy of page 27. Present the following directions.
Look at Row 1.

- Write a *Z* on the middle ball and a *Y* on the last ball.

- Draw a horizontal line through all three balls. Then, make a check mark above the first ball.

- Draw a vertical line between the second and third balls and a horizontal line to the right of the last ball.

Look at Row 2.

- Draw a line above the circle and cross out the triangle.

- Write the letter *G* in the square. Then, draw a line under the *G*.

- Draw a line from the circle to the triangle and write the number *1* to the right of the triangle.

Look at Row 3.

- Write the letter *P* in front of the pig and the letter *S* in the back of the shoe.

- Draw an arrow pointing to the heel of the shoe and circle the pig's tail.

- Draw a box around the pig's left ear and connect the pig and the shoe with a curved line.

Following Directions

Listen carefully to the directions for each row.

Row 1

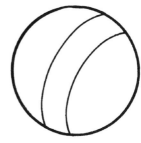 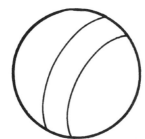 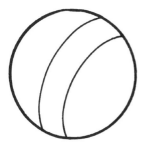

Row 2

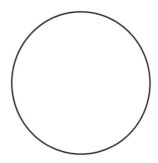  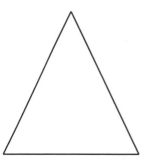

Row 3

Gross-Motor Response

Materials: telephone, paper, wastebasket

1. Sit on the floor.
2. Touch your hair.
3. Now, stand up.
4. Count to five.
5. Walk to the telephone.
6. Show me a big smile.
7. Pick up a piece of paper.
8. Now, take a very deep breath.
9. Throw the paper into the wastebasket.
10. Sit down.

Fine-Motor Response

Give the student a copy of page 29. Present the following directions.

Look at Row 1.

• Write the letter *O* in the second triangle and the number *7* in the first triangle.

• Draw a line above the first triangle and draw a wiggly line between the two triangles.

• Draw a small triangle to the left of the first triangle. Then, draw a big rectangle around everything.

Look at Row 2.

• Write the letter *S* in the first square and the number *3* between the squares.

• Draw a line above the second square and an arrow below the first square.

• Draw a line from the bottom of the first square to the top of the second square and make two dots in the second square.

Look at Row 3.

• Draw a circle around the symbol that indicates a question and underline the symbol that indicates addition.

• Write the number *3* to the left of the plus sign and the number *2* to the right of the plus sign.

• To the left of the check mark, make an equal sign. Then, write the number *5* to the right of the check mark.

Following Directions

Name _____

Listen carefully to the directions for each row.

Row 1

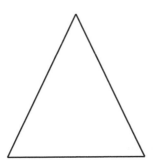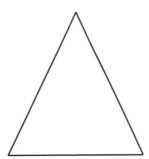

Row 2

Row 3

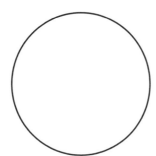

Gross-Motor Response

Materials: something blue, clock, watch

1. Point to the door and then to the ceiling.
2. Stand on one foot. Then, stand on the other.
3. Walk to the door and open it.
4. Touch your toes and then your nose.
5. Raise your hand and your foot.
6. Run back to your seat and sit down.
7. Name something that is blue and show it to me.
8. Show me your fingernails and count your fingers.
9. Sing the birthday song and then hum it.
10. Name the numbers on the clock. Then, look at my watch.

Fine-Motor Response

Give the student a copy of page 31. Present the following directions.

Look at Row 1.

- Shade in the leaves of the flowers. Then, draw a line from the flower to the bottle and draw a cap on the bottle.

- Draw a heart around the flower, a square around the bottle, and a diamond around the candle.

- Cross out the flame on the candle, write the letter *B* on the bottle, and write the letter *F* above the flower.

Look at Row 2.

- Add a leaf to the flower, draw an arrow pointing toward the pig, and draw a line under the pig.

- Draw a diamond to the left of the pig and a square to the right of the flower. Then, make a check mark above the flower.

- Cross out the pig's snout. Then, write the number *1* on the pig's mouth and the number *2* on the flower.

Look at Row 3.

- Draw an apple in the tree, write the letter *T* to the right of the letter *S*, and give the home a chimney.

- Draw a window on the house, a knob on the door, and a flower under the tree.

- Write an *O* to the right of the *T*. Then, put a *P* to the right of the *O*. Then, write the word *stop* between the tree and the house.

Following Directions

Name _____

Listen carefully to the directions for each row.

Row 1

Row 2

Row 3

S

Gross-Motor Response

Materials: pictures, clock

1. Touch your chin and your cheeks.
2. Show me your teeth. Then, open your mouth.
3. Tell me your name and your age.
4. Show me a picture and tell me what you see.
5. Tap your foot and click your tongue.
6. Hop to the door and knock on it.
7. Now, close the door and turn around.
8. Show me your thumbs and wiggle them.
9. Wiggle your fingers and raise your hands.
10. Look at the clock and tell me where it is.

Fine-Motor Response

Give the student a copy of page 33. Present the following directions.

Look at Row 1.

- Make a plus sign in the square and an equal sign in the circle. Then, write the number *7* to the right of the circle.

- Write the fourth letter of the alphabet in the triangle and draw a line above the square. Then, draw a diamond around the number *7*.

- Draw a vertical line to the left of the triangle. Then, make a check mark above the number *2* and cross out the number *2*.

Look at Row 2.

- Draw a hat on the boy. Then, give him two ears and a pair of glasses.

- Give the girl a pair of glasses. Draw a necklace under her chin and a bow in her hair.

- Write the letter *B* to the left of the girl, the letter *O* between the boy and the girl, and the letter *Y* to the right of the boy.

Look at Row 3.

- Draw a box around the apple, cross out the banana, and circle the triangle.

- Draw a smaller triangle inside the larger triangle, draw a line under the apple, and write the number *3* between the banana and the triangle.

- Write the letter *S* in the apple and the letter *O* between the apple and the banana. Then, write the word *so* to the right of the triangle.

Following Directions

Name _____

Listen carefully to the directions for each row.

Row 1

  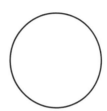 2

Row 2

Row 3

  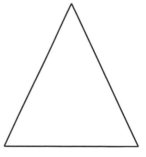

Gross-Motor Response

Materials: pencil, calendar, pencil sharpener

1. Walk to the door and knock on it.
2. Stick out your tongue and wiggle it.
3. Sit down and fold your arms.
4. Sharpen the pencil and put in on the desk.
5. Rest your head on the desk and lift your foot.
6. Show me the calendar and tell me where it is.
7. Tell me the names of your best friend and your teacher.
8. Sit in your chair and say your name.
9. Close your mouth and open it quickly.
10. Look at your shoes and then look at your socks.

Fine-Motor Response

Give the student a copy of page 35. Present the following directions.

Look at Row 1.

- Cross out the first small heart, make a check mark in the second small heart, and draw a line under the large heart.

- Divide the large heart in half and write the number *1* in each half. Then, make a plus sign between the numbers.

- Write the number *2* above the large heart. Then, write the letter *H* above the first small heart and the letter *T* above the second small heart.

Look at Row 2.

- Draw a horizontal line straight across the three triangles so they are connected. Then, make a check mark in the first triangle and also the third triangle.

- Write the word *yes* between the first and second triangles. Then, write the word *no* between the second and third triangles and circle the word *no*.

- Write the number *2* in the middle triangle. Then, draw a line under the first triangle and cross out the last triangle.

Look at Row 3.

- Write an *X* in the triangle. Then, divide the triangle in half and underline it.

- Draw a box around the rabbit's ears. Then, make a check mark in his right ear and a check mark in his left ear.

- Make a minus sign to the left of the triangle, a plus sign between the triangle and the rabbit, and a multiplication sign to the right of the rabbit.

Following Directions

Name _____

Listen carefully to the directions for each row.

Row 1

Row 2

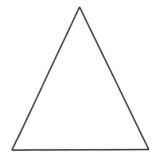 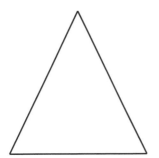 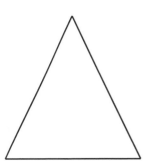

Row 3

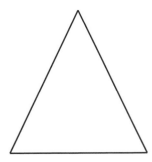 

Gross-Motor Response

Materials: books, paper, pencil, calendar

1. Pick up a book and show me the title.
2. Give me a piece of paper and then a pencil.
3. Open the door and look outside.
4. Knock on the door and turn the doorknob.
5. Tell me today's day and date.
6. Look out the door again and say "Hello."
7. Snap your fingers and hum.
8. Open a book and tell me the page number.
9. Close the book and tell me the title.
10. Clap your hands and nod your head.

Fine-Motor Response

Give the student a copy of page 37. Present the following directions.

Look at Row 1.

- Draw a circle in the first triangle, a diamond in the second triangle, and a triangle in the large square.

- Make a check mark above the small square, cross out the second triangle, and draw a line under the first triangle.

- Draw a line from the large square to the first triangle and extend it to the second triangle. Then, draw a vertical line to the left of the large square.

Look at Row 2.

- Draw a line from the cat to the ball. Then, shade in the band on the ball and write the letter *C* above the cup.

- Write the number *1* in the ball, circle the cat's ears, and cross out the cup.

- Write the number *2* to the left of the cat and the number *4* to the right of the cat. Then, draw a diamond around the ball.

Look at Row 3.

- Divide the square in half with a diagonal line, divide the triangle in half with a vertical line, and divide the hexagon in half with a horizontal line.

- Make a check mark in the hexagon, cross out the triangle, and underline the square.

- Write the letter *J* to the left of the square, write the number *4* between the triangle and the hexagon, and write a plus sign in the hexagon.

Following Directions

Name _____

Listen carefully to the directions for each row.

Row 1

 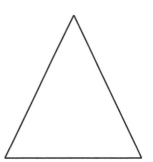 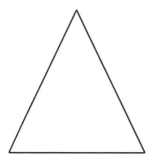

Row 2

  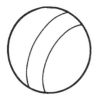

Row 3

 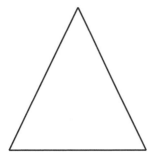 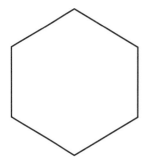

Gross-Motor Response

Materials: books, paper, telephone

1. Give a book to me and then put it on the table.
2. Rip a piece of paper and then crumple it up.
3. Walk to the telephone and dial your number.
4. Now, put your hands on the table and tap them.
5. Whisper your name and the day of the week.
6. Show me how you yawn and tell me how you feel.
7. Open a book and put it on the floor.
8. Close your eyes and your mouth.
9. Show me how you stretch and groan.
10. Open your eyes and look at me.

Fine-Motor Response

Give the student a copy of page 39. Present the following directions.

Look at Row 1.

- Underline the rectangle, make a check mark above the square, and cross out the second circle.

- Write the number *5* in the rectangle, make a plus sign between the rectangle and the first circle, and write the number *4* in the first circle.

- Make an equal sign between the first circle and the square, write the number *9* in the square, and make an exclamation mark to the right of the square.

Look at Row 2.

- From the middle of the clock, draw a long arrow pointing toward the *12* and a short arrow pointing toward the *3*. Then, write the number *4* in the clock.

- Write *5 + 1* in the square, make an equal sign between the square and the triangle, and write the number *6* in the triangle.

- Draw a horizontal line above the clock and a diagonal line between the clock and the square.

Look at Row 3.

- Make a question mark in the middle diamond, an exclamation mark in the last diamond, and a comma in the first diamond.

- Write a *5* to the left of the first diamond, a plus sign between the first and second diamonds, and another *5* between the second and third diamonds.

- Cross out the last diamond, underline the first diamond, and draw a line above the second diamond.

Following Directions

Name _____

Listen carefully to the directions for each row.

Row 1

 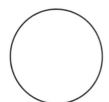  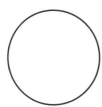

Row 2

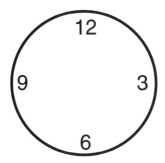  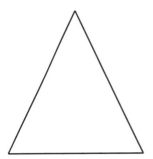

Row 3

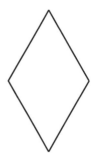 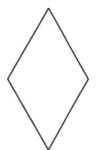 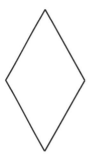

Gross-Motor Response

Materials: paper, wastebasket

1. Walk around the table and then, sit down.
2. Touch your hair and your knees.
3. Pick up a piece of paper and crumple it into a ball.
4. Throw the paper away and sit down.
5. Sit up straight and look at the door.
6. Take a deep breath and hold it.
7. Let your breath out and say "Ahh."
8. Stand up and salute like a soldier.
9. Count to five and say "High five!"
10. Point to the floor and then to the ceiling.

Fine-Motor Response

Give the student a copy of page 41. Present the following directions.

Look at Row 1.

- Write the number *8* above the first pie, the number *4* above the second pie, and the number *6* above the third pie.

- Draw a box around the first pie, draw a knife to the right of the middle pie, and add two slices to the last pie.

- Make a plus sign between the *8* and the *4*, another plus sign between the *4* and the *6*, and an equal sign to the right of the *6*.

Look at Row 2.

- Shade in the first small heart, draw a box around the second small heart, and write the number *5* in the middle of the large heart.

- Draw a dotted line to connect the two small hearts. Then, draw a vertical line to the left of the large heart.

- Draw a circle around the first small heart. Then, write the letter *G* above the large heart.

Look at Row 3.

- Cross out the small circle, write a period in the large circle, and write the word *go* in the square.

- Write the number *2* in the triangle and the number *3* between the triangle and the square. Then, draw a vertical line between the square and the large circle.

- Connect the triangle and the square with a straight line, draw an arrow pointing to the large circle, and draw a diamond around the small circle.

Following Directions

Name _____

Listen carefully to the directions for each row.

Row 1

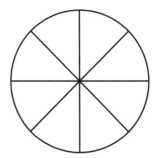 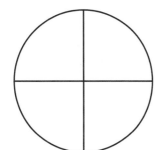 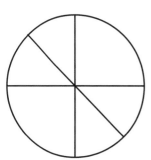

Row 2

Row 3

  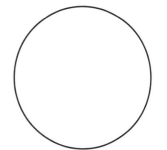

Gross-Motor Response

Materials: telephone, wastebasket, pencil, pen, book, paper

1. Sit on the floor and count to three.
2. Tell me your birthday and how old you will be.
3. Point to a word on a book and spell it.
4. Show me a pencil and then a pen.
5. Cover your ears and then your eyes.
6. Show me a big smile and tell me how you feel.
7. Throw a piece of paper to me and then, put it in the wastebasket.
8. Point to the telephone and tell me your phone number.
9. Put your hands together and set them on your lap.
10. Stand up and then, turn around.

Fine-Motor Response

Give the student a copy of page 43. Present the following directions.

Look at Row 1.

- Divide the first triangle in half with a vertical line and divide the second triangle in half with a horizontal line. Then, draw a circle between the two triangles.

- Draw a square to the left of the first triangle and a diamond to the right of the second triangle. Underline both triangles.

- Write the number *2* above the first triangle, the number *3* above the second triangle, and the number *5* under the diamond.

Look at Row 2.

- Cross out the glass that is empty and make a check mark in the glass that is almost full. Then, shade in the liquid for the glass that is almost empty.

- In the empty glass, draw a water line that shows a glass half full of water. Draw a few drops of water to the left of that glass. Then, draw a line under that glass.

- Shade in the empty area for the middle glass, write the number *5* between the second and third glasses, and draw a line from the first to the last glass.

Look at Row 3.

- Write the letter *T* in the triangle, the letter that follows *O* in the square, and the last letter of the alphabet in the circle.

- Write the number after *3* between the circle and the square and the number after *8* between the square and the triangle. Then, draw a diamond to the right of the triangle.

- Underline the *4,* draw a line over the *9,* and write a *2* in the diamond.

Following Directions

Name _____

Listen carefully to the directions for each row.

Row 1

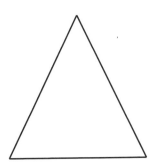 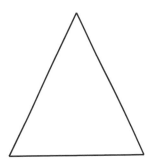

Row 2

Row 3

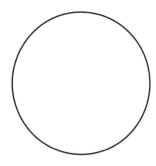  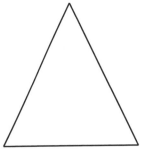

Gross-Motor Response

Materials: pencil, paper

1. Think of an animal that lays eggs. Then, give me clues so I can guess what it is. Finally, write its name on a piece of paper.

2. Bend to one side at your waist. Then, bend forward at your waist. Then, stand up straight.

3. Blink your eyes first, pat your cheek second, and touch your shoulder third.

4. Take off your shoes and put them on the table. Then, describe your shoes.

5. Pretend you are a teapot; make your arm into a spout and pour yourself out.

Fine-Motor Response

Give the student a copy of page 45. Present the following directions.

Look at Row 1.

- Underline the figure that is most similar to a cube and divide it in half, using a diagonal line from the upper-left corner to the lower-right corner.

- Draw a line from the upper-right corner of the box to the lower-right corner of the rectangle, going above the circle and below the octagon.

- Using a dotted line, connect the circle and octagon. Then, write the number that follows *2* in the rectangle.

Look at Row 2.

- Make a check mark above the largest even number and underline the smallest odd number.

- Write the symbol that indicates subtraction between the last two numbers. Then, write the equal sign to the right of the last number.

- Complete the equation for subtraction and write the answer in the diamond.

Look at Row 3.

- Draw a line from the leaves on the tree to the lowest thorn on the rose and add a petal to the rose.

- Draw a rectangle around the handle of the brush and a box around the leaves of the rose.

- Write the letter *T* on the trunk of the tree and the letter *R* on the rose blossom.

Following Directions

Name _____

Listen carefully to the directions for each row.

Row 1

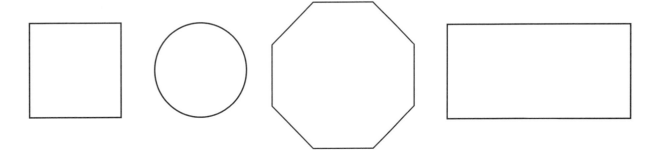

Row 2

5   18   21   9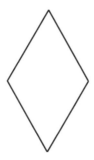

Row 3

Gross-Motor Response

Materials: pencil, paper, crayons (including a red one), scissors

1. Pretend to play the piano. Be sure to turn the pages and don't look at your fingers.

2. Get a piece of paper and a pencil and write your name.

3. Use a red crayon to draw a line on a piece of paper. Then, cut on the line with the scissors.

4. Tell me your middle name, then tell me how old you are, and finally, tell me something you like to do.

5. Draw a shape in the air. Don't tell me what it is, and I'll take a guess.

Fine-Motor Response

Give the student a copy of page 47. Present the following directions.

Look at Row 1.

• Write any odd number in the part of the rectangle that is inside the square and make a check mark in the upper-right corner of the square.

• Write an even number in the highest point of the star and write the sum of *5 + 5* in the part of the rectangle that is outside the square.

• Make a question mark in the lower-right corner of the square and, using a vertical line, divide the square in half.

Look at Row 2.

• Connect the strings of the last two balloons with a dotted line. Write the word that tells what you do when you are hungry in the first balloon.

• At the bottom of the string of the first balloon, draw a rock. Then, draw a pin almost ready to stick into the same balloon.

• Write the sum of *9 + 8* in the middle balloon and write the number that is equal to *7 - 6* in the last balloon.

Look at Row 3.

• Draw a straight line to connect the bottoms of any two of the three circles. Then, divide the first circle in half with a horizontal line.

• Write the number *4* in the top half of the first circle and the number *9* in the bottom half of the first circle.

• Write the letter after *D* in the second circle, using lowercase. Then, write the letter that comes before *F* in the last circle, using uppercase.

Following Directions

Name _____

Listen carefully to the directions for each row.

Row 1

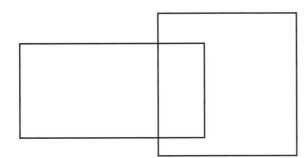

Row 2

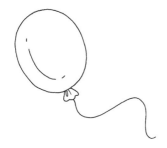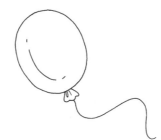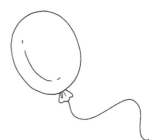

Row 3

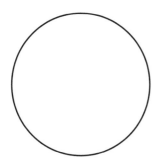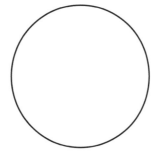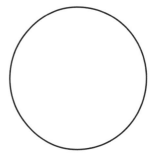

Gross-Motor Response

Materials: chalkboard, chalk, calendar, paper, envelope

1. Take off your shoe. Wiggle your toes and then, wiggle your fingers.

2. Go to the chalkboard, write today's date, and say it out loud.

3. Stretch to try to touch the ceiling. Then, bend down and try to touch the floor. Finally, stretch your arms to each side and try to touch the walls.

4. Write a word on my back with your finger; the word should begin with *S* and should have four or five letters.

5. Fold a piece of paper. Put in into an envelope and seal it.

Fine-Motor Response

Give the student a copy of page 49. Present the following directions.

Look at Row 1.

- Cross out the *S* in the word with three letters and underline the double vowel.

- Circle the blend and add a letter to the word *go* to make a new word.

- Cross out the word with the most letters and circle the word that tells you what to do with a chair.

Look at Row 2.

- Cross out the figure that appears only once. Then, in the last three-sided figure, write the number that is equal to *2 + 2*.

- At the top of the first circle, write the number *1*. At the bottom of the second circle, write the letter that comes between *M* and *O*.

- Make a check mark in the lower-left corner of the first triangle. Then, make another check mark in the lower point of the diamond.

Look at Row 3.

- Cross out the thing that is cold. Then, write an *F* above the thing that grows on trees.

- Write the label for the last object to the right of that object. Then, circle the vowels.

- Choose a number between *3* and *7* and write it above the ice cream cone.

Following Directions

Listen carefully to the directions for each row.

Row 1

go   eat   sit   stop

Row 2

 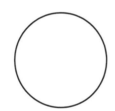 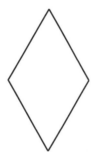 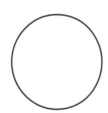 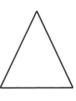

Row 3

Gross-Motor Response

Materials: paper clip, envelope, pencil

1. Name a flower. Then, name a toy. Finally, name your favorite subject.

2. Pretend to be a baby. Drink your bottle and then, crawl on the floor.

3. Put the paper clip on the table, put the envelope in a drawer, and tell me the color of the pencil.

4. Recite the alphabet. Then, tell me a word that begins with the letter *F* and write it in the air.

5. Shake my hand, introduce yourself, and ask me a question.

Fine-Motor Response

Give the student a copy of page 51. Present the following directions.

Look at Row 1.

- Write the first letter of the second word on the first line and the second letter of the first word on the second line.

- Write the third letter of the first word on the third line. Then, write the new word, using lowercase letters, to the right of the second word.

- Cross out the last two letters of the first word and write that new word, using uppercase letters, to the left of the first word.

Look at Row 2.

- Add one circle to the middle rectangle. Then, below that rectangle, write the number that represents the total number of circles in the middle rectangle.

- Count the circles in the first and third rectangles and add them together. Write your answer to the right of the last rectangle.

- Cross out one circle from each rectangle. Then, write the total number of circles remaining to the left of the first rectangle.

Look at Row 3.

- Draw a line from the top of the star to the bottom of the second circle, going through the box and under the first circle.

- Using a vertical line, separate the two circles. Then, write the number *7* in the circle on the left.

- Make a check mark on the highest point of the star and write the letter *S* in the bottom-left corner of the square.

Following Directions

Listen carefully to the directions for each row.

Row 1

wagon   bike

—   —   —

Row 2

 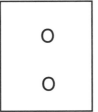

Row 3

  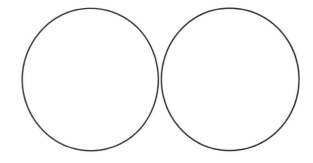

Gross-Motor Response

Materials: tape roll, pen, envelope, paper clip

1. Bring me a roll of tape, a pen, and an envelope.

2. Describe something in the kitchen. Don't tell me what it is; let me guess.

3. Walk to the desk, get a paper clip, and give it to me.

4. Tell me the color of grass. Then, tell me the color of the sky. Then, tell me the color of milk.

5. Tell me what a pretzel tastes like, how ice cream feels, and what it sounds like when you bite into an apple.

Fine-Motor Response

Give the student a copy of page 53. Present the following directions.

Look at Row 1.

- Write the initial for your last name in the widest part of the spoon and circle the double vowels in the word *seek*.

- Write the sum of *2 + 3* in the square and the number that comes after *21* in the circle.

- Write a vowel, but not *E*, between the square and the circle. Then, cross out the widest part of the spoon.

Look at Row 2.

- Draw a line under the highest number. Then, draw a line connecting that number to the arrow pointing up.

- Make a check mark under the arrow pointing down. Then, draw a line to connect that arrow with the smallest number.

- Make the sign that represents addition between the *9* and the *2*. Then, write that sum in a circle to the right of the *2*.

Look at Row 3.

- Make a check mark on the highest point of the first star and underline the star that is separated from the first star by a flower.

- Draw a box around the part of the flower that smells good and write the letter *S* on the upper-left point of the last star.

- Cross out the star that has a letter on it and write the same letter on the lower-right point of the first star.

Following Directions

Name _____

Listen carefully to the directions for each row.

Row 1

  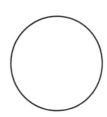 seek

Row 2

  9 2

Row 3

Gross-Motor Response

Materials: calendar

1. Look at the calendar and tell me the day and date. Don't forget to tell me the year.

2. Take off your shoes and stand on your toes. Then, sit down.

3. Tell me the name of your favorite food, what it looks like, and how it tastes.

4. Wait for me to cover my ears. Then, whisper a word and ask me to tell you what you said.

5. Touch your eyes with one hand, touch your tummy with your other hand, and then stand up.

Fine-Motor Response

Give the student a copy of page 55. Present the following directions.

Look at Row 1.

• Label the first triangle by writing an uppercase *T* to the left of it. Then, label the large circle by writing an uppercase *C* in the middle of it.

• Using a vertical line, divide each triangle in half. Using a horizontal line, divide each circle in half.

• In the upper half of the small circle, make a period. On the right side of the small triangle, make a comma.

Look at Row 2.

• Draw a leaf on the trunk of the tree and make a check mark on the number that is opposite the *3* on the clock.

• Draw a bee on a petal of the flower and write the number that comes before *6* on the clock.

• Draw a vertical line between the clock and the tree. Then, write a *V* on the lower end to turn it into a downward-pointing arrow.

Look at Row 3.

• Write the letter *A* in the upper-right corner of the rectangle. Then, write the letter *P* in the upper corner of the diamond.

• Add another letter *P* in the lower corner of the diamond and write the letter *L* in the lower-left corner of the square.

• Write the letter *E* in the highest point of the triangle. Then, to the right of the triangle, draw a picture to match what the letters spell.

Following Directions

Name _____

Listen carefully to the directions for each row.

Row 1

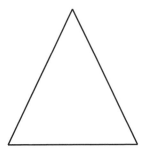 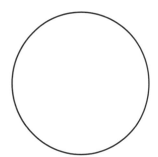

Row 2

 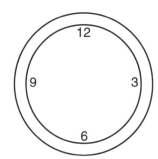 

Row 3

 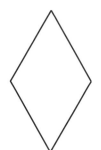  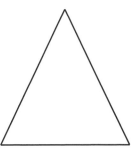

Central Auditory Processing Kit, Book 3
Auditory Figure-Ground—Following Directions   55

Gross-Motor Response

Materials: pencil, pencil sharpener, box of crayons, bag, paper

1. First, tell me your favorite color. Second, tell me something you have with that color. Third, tell me something you would like to have with that color.

2. Get a pencil from the desk. Sharpen it and then, write three numbers on a piece of paper.

3. Describe something in your bedroom, but don't tell me what it is. Let me guess.

4. Take the box of crayons, pull out red and yellow, and give the box back to me.

5. Get the bag and put the pencil in it. Then, close the bag.

Fine-Motor Response

Give the student a copy of page 57. Present the following directions.

Look at Row 1.

- Decide what the sum of *6 + 4* equals. Then, write that equation above the number.

- Decide what answer you get when you subtract *3* from *10* and write that equation above the number.

- Decide what odd number comes after the number *3*. Then, write that number to the right of the *3*.

Look at Row 2.

- Make a check mark on the chair that has a ball in back of it. Then, circle the chair to the right of the chair with a ball in front of it.

- Find the chair with a ball on the seat. Then, draw another ball under the seat.

- Using a solid line, connect the top of the chair that has the ball on the seat to the front leg of the chair that has a ball in front of it.

Look at Row 3.

- Draw a vertical line to close the first figure. Then, extend the line upward to form the lowercase letter *D*.

- Using a dotted line, connect the last two circles. Using a solid line, close the third circle.

- Write the number *5* in the circle on the left and the number *6* on the dotted line that's between the circles.

Following Directions

Name _____

Listen carefully to the directions for each row.

Row 1

Row 2

   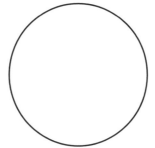   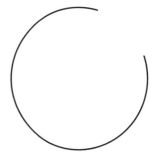

Row 3

Gross-Motor Response

Materials: calendar, sticky notes

1. Take off your right shoe, place it near the lower-left corner of the desk, and then describe it in a whispered voice.
2. Pretend you are a baby frog. Hop around the table twice and say "Ribbit" with a baby-frog voice.
3. Tell me the time you eat breakfast on Sundays. Then, tell me the time you eat dinner on Fridays. Finally, tell me the time you eat lunch at school.
4. Look at the calendar to find the last day of school. Tell me the day and date. Then, write it on a sticky note so we won't forget.
5. First, write a number between *1* and *5* in the air. Then, write a letter between *A* and *G* in the air. Finally, tell me what you wrote, beginning with the letter.

Fine-Motor Response

Give the student a copy of page 59. Present the following directions.

Look at Row 1.

- Cross out the capital letter of the first school day of the week. Circle the months that begin with that same letter. Finally, underline the fifth month of the year.

- Underline the part of the word that's the same for each weekday. Then, think of a symbol for the month of April and draw it under that word.

- Think of another way to spell *Friday* and write it below that word. Then, think of something that can be fried and draw it above the word *Friday*.

Look at Row 2.

- Look at the first number pattern and decide what number comes after the number *5*. Then, write that number, separating it from the *5* with a dash.

- Write the numbers between *10* and *15* under the first number pattern. Use a pencil and separate each number by a dash.

- Below the second number pattern, write the number that should come before the *6*. Then, write the two numbers that should come after the *8*.

Look at Row 3.

- Look at the pattern of colors for the second string of beads and decide what color would come next if a third bead were added. Add that bead.

- In the first string of beads, color the fourth bead with the color needed to continue the pattern. Then, add a fifth bead to continue the pattern.

- Cross out the third bead on the third string and add a bead at the front of the string. Decide what color it should be.

Following Directions

Name _____

Listen carefully to the directions for each row.

Row 1

Monday   April   Friday   August   May

Row 2

1-3-5   6-8   5-10-15-20

Row 3

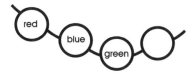   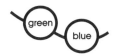   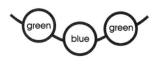

Gross-Motor Response

Materials: paper, pencil or pen

1. Pretend you are an elephant. Walk around the room slowly and swing your trunk to the right only.
2. Recite the alphabet as quickly as you can. Then, tell me the name of an appliance that begins with the letter *F*. Finally, write the letter *F* in the air with your smallest finger.
3. Tell me the color of grass in the winter. Then, tell me the color of the sky at night. Then, tell me the color of a strawberry shake.
4. Take a deep breath through your nose and hold it for three seconds while you pretend to swim underwater. Then, let your breath out as you say "Ahh" loudly.
5. Spell your first name aloud. Then, write your last name on the bottom half of a piece of paper. Finally, say your full name aloud.

Fine-Motor Response

Give the student a copy of page 61. Present the following directions.

Look at Row 1.

* Make a plus sign between the second and third numbers and an equal sign to the right of the third number. Circle the fourth number with a red marker.

* Draw a line under the equation you just finished. Then, draw a diagonal line to the right of the number *13* and write the number that comes after it.

* Above the number *1*, draw a body part you have only one of. Then, write the letter that body part begins with under the number *1* with a black pen.

Look at Row 2.

* In the middle clock, the short hand is pointing to the number that comes after *3* and the long hand is pointing to the number that comes between *9* and *11*. Write these numbers on the clock.

* Using a blue pen, show 2:00 in the first clock and 7:00 in the third clock. Write in the numbers and draw the clock hands.

* Fill in the numbers between *3* and *6* in the first clock and between *9* and *12* in the third clock. Then, go to the middle clock and write the *2* where it belongs.

Look at Row 3.

* Separate the letters *M* and *N* with a curvy, vertical line. Then, draw a horizontal line through the middle of the *B*. Connect the *S* to the *R*, using an arched line.

* Under the *R*, write the word that completes this sentence: "I ran in the ___." It rhymes with *face*. Then, put the letters *A* and *R* in front of the *M* and draw a small picture of that word underneath it.

* Write the letter *U* between the *B* and the *S*. Put brackets around those three letters. Then, rewrite the word underneath, using lowercase letters.

Following Directions

Listen carefully to the directions for each row.

Row 1

1   3   6   9   13

Row 2

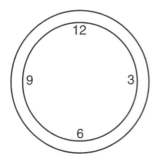  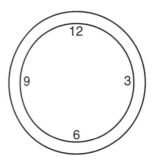

Row 3

M N B S O R

Gross-Motor Response

Materials: pencils (one red); thick, blue book; other book(s); magazine; bag

1. Put the red pencil in the bag. Then, close the bag tightly and put it under the chair.

2. Count to *5* backwards from *10*, turn around twice, and skip around the table three times.

3. Open the thick, blue book first. Then, open the magazine to the table of contents. Then, show me page twelve in the book.

4. Shake my hand as though you are very glad to see me. Then, introduce yourself and a friend to me. Finally, ask me a question about where I live.

5. Tell me the name of an animated movie you have seen. Next, whistle a tune from that movie. Then, tell me your favorite character from the movie.

Fine-Motor Response

Give the student a copy of page 63. Present the following directions.

Look at Row 1.

*   Draw a dotted line from the first domino to the last domino. Begin the line at either side of the first domino and end on the right side of the last domino. Then, shade in both dominos with a yellow crayon.

*   Cross out the third domino and, below the last domino, draw another domino that is identical to the second one. Then, with an orange crayon, shade in the domino that you drew.

*   Write the number of dots in each domino above each domino. Then, make a plus sign between each of the numbers and write the sum to the right of the last domino.

Look at Row 2.

*   Write the numbers for each inch under the appropriate lines. Then, think of another word to use for *twelve* when you're thinking about doughnuts or eggs. Write that word to the right of the ruler.

*   Pretend you are a carpenter and you need to measure two pieces of wood. One piece is 6" long and the other is 8" long. What is your total length of wood?

*   Write the total length under the ruler after you have highlighted the 6" mark and the 8" mark with your yellow marker. Use the symbol for inches rather than the word *inches*.

Look at Row 3.

*   Make a check mark above the animal with the longest ears. Draw a horizontal line under the cat's tail and cross out the pig's snout.

*   Write the letter *C* on the cat's body. Write the letter *R* on the rabbit's left ear. Write the letter *P* under the pig's chin.

*   Before you shade the pig's face with a pink crayon, lightly color the rabbit's ears with the same crayon. Then, color the cat's mouth pink as well.

Following Directions

Name _____

Listen carefully to the directions for each row.

Row 1

  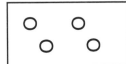 

Row 2

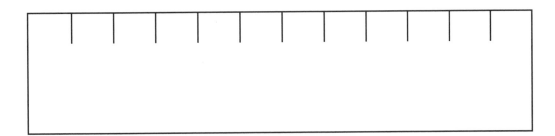

Row 3

Level 4: Radio Talk Shows, *continued*

Gross-Motor Response

Materials: scarf, ball, large and small paper clips, new pencil, black pen, paper

1. Wait for me to cover my ears with this scarf. Then, whisper a three-syllable word and ask me what you said after four seconds.
2. Move your chair to the left of the door. Next, hide the ball inside of something in this room. Then, give me three clues so I can find it.
3. Walk quickly to the desk, get a large paper clip, and put it in my right hand.
4. First, hum "Row, Row, Row Your Boat" with a loud voice. Second, sing the same song quietly. Third, write the word *boat* in the air, using only lowercase letters.
5. Tap on the table five times with your left pointer finger. Then, tap three times with the brand new pencil. Finally, tap once with the black pen.

Fine-Motor Response

Give the student a copy of page 65. Present the following directions.

Look at Row 1.

- Cross out the letter *E* in the first and second words and write that letter two times in the third circle, separating each *E* with a comma.
- Find the remaining two vowels and write one in the first circle, using a red pen, and the other in the second circle, using a black pen. Cross out the vowels in the words when you're done writing.
- Write the two consonants that are together in the fourth circle. Then, cross out those letters in the word where you found them. Finally, tell me a simple word that begins with the sound of *B*.

Look at Row 2.

- With a solid, black line, connect the triangle that is in a triangle to the triangle that stands alone. Then, shade in both triangles lightly with the black crayon so they look gray.
- With a dotted, green line, connect the circle that is in a triangle to the circle that stands alone. Then, shade in both circles lightly, using a green crayon.
- Write the letters *T* and *D* in the diamond that is in a triangle. Write the letter *D* in the diamond that stands alone. Then, shade in both diamonds with an orange crayon.

Look at Row 3.

- Make a check mark under the smallest number in the sixties. Separate the two digits in the first number with a vertical dotted line and cross out the second of the two numbers in the number *41*.
- Make a plus sign between the *6* and the *8* in the number *68*. Add those two numbers together and write the sum underneath.
- Draw a circle around the second digit of the number *47*. Before you underline number *41*, underline the number in the circle.

Following Directions

Listen carefully to the directions for each row.

Row 1

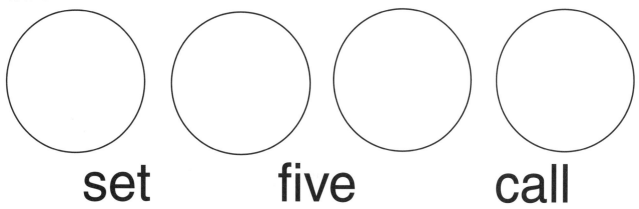

set   five   call

Row 2

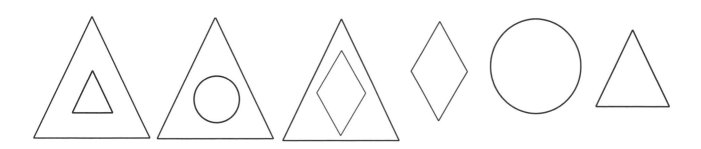

Row 3

27   62   68   47   41

Gross-Motor Response

Materials: 3 pieces construction paper; pebble; markers, including black; pencils, including red; green paper; magazine with recipes; paper strips

1. Arrange the pieces of construction paper for a hopscotch grid. Then, use the black marker to number each square. Finally, take the pebble and toss it onto one of the squares.
2. Think of something in your room that is green. Draw it on a green piece of paper and whisper what it is in my left ear.
3. Get a small strip of paper and a red pencil. Write your name in uppercase letters.
4. First, show me a page in the magazine that gives you a recipe. Second, show me a page that has an advertisement. Third, tell me who likes to read this magazine in your home.
5. Describe something in the kitchen in the appliance category. Don't tell me what it is unless I ask you to. Be sure to give me three clues.

Fine-Motor Response

Give the student a copy of page 67. Present the following directions.

Look at Row 1.

- Separate the last three letters from the first three with one wavy line. Then, draw a star on the last letter and a diamond on the first letter.
- Cross out the second letter to the right of the letter *C*. Draw a horizontal arrow between the *C* and the *E*, pointing it toward the E.
- After the letter *U*, write the letter that comes before *D* but after *B*. Use a lowercase form and a red pencil.

Look at Row 2.

- Shade in the triangle that is in the square. Draw a short, horizontal line above the square with a circle in it. Make a check mark in the circle that is in a square.
- Write the number *1* in the center of the diamond that is in a square. Write a number *2* in the diamond that is next to the diamond in a square. Then, connect the two diamonds with a solid, green line.
- Draw a dotted, blue line from the diamond in a square to the circle that stands alone, going above all the shapes that lie between them, to form a nice arch.

Look at Row 3.

- Write the number *3002* above the door of the house. Draw in a curb on the street and write the same number on the curb.
- Write the word *saw* under that tool, using lowercase, black letters. Then, mark a spot on the tree trunk with a blue marker where you would put that saw to cut down a tree.
- Draw in one branch on the tree. Make a nest on that branch and then, put three pink eggs in the nest.

Following Directions

Listen carefully to the directions for each row.

Row 1

C E J P U S

Row 2

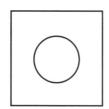   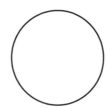

Row 3

Gross-Motor Response

Materials: chalkboard

1. Bend to the right at the waist and hold for three seconds. Then, bend to the left at your waist and hold for three seconds. Finally, bend forward at your waist and hold for three seconds.
2. Pretend you are a teapot. Make your left arm into a spout and pour tea into three cups.
3. Describe something in your bedroom that is rectangular. Give me three clues. Then, wait four seconds before you ask me to make a guess.
4. Think of the names of two girls that begin with the letter P. Write them on the board, using uppercase letters. Then, read them aloud with a quiet voice.
5. First, I want you to stand up like a soldier. Then, march to the door and say "Hi" with a booming voice.

Fine-Motor Response

Give the student a copy of page 69. Present the following directions.

Look at Row 1.

- Draw a red heart around the second letter. Draw a blue diamond around the letter that comes before *R* and a yellow circle around the last letter of the alphabet.
- Draw a line under the letter *B,* using an orange marker. Then, write the word that rhymes with *toy* and has *B* as its first letter over the letter *B*.
- Draw a vertical line to the right of the letter *F*. Then, write the letter *F* two times next to the vertical line, once in the lowercase form with your green crayon and once in the uppercase form with your brown crayon.

Look at Row 2.

- Think of the last month of the year. Then, write the first letter of that month in the first box. Use an uppercase form and a black marker.
- When the colors blue and green are mixed together, they make a new color. Write this new color in the second box, using the same color marker as the color name you are writing. If you're not sure of the new color, guess.
- Draw a line under the color word that is used for water. Draw a line above the color word that is used for the sun. Then, highlight each word with its matching color.

Look at Row 3.

- Draw a black line from the second-to-last triangle to the second *M* in the name *Sammie*. Then, underline that letter, being sure to use a color other than black.
- Cross out the letter that is repeated three times. Add a new letter or letters to the last word to create another word. Add a new letter or letters to *Sa* to create a new word.
- Highlight the new letters with your yellow marker. Then, draw a blue circle around each new word you created. Then, rewrite those words in the first and last triangles.

Following Directions

Listen carefully to the directions for each row.

Row 1

B R Q Z F

Row 2

 blue  yellow

Row 3

Sammie   Tom

Gross-Motor Response

Materials: book, paper, pencil

1. Tell me one thing you learned in science last week. Tell me how knowing this new information will help you in life, and tell me what you would like to learn in science next.
2. Think of a number between *5* and *10*. Write it in a book with your pointer finger and tell me to guess what you wrote after three seconds.
3. Take off your right shoe and stand on your toes for five seconds. Then, sit down next to me.
4. Describe one corner of your room. Then, tell me what you have on the floor of your closet. Finally, tell me what you have in the top drawer of your dresser.
5. Think of a food word that begins with *M*. Then, write it on the back of a piece of paper and tell me to read it with a quiet voice.

Fine-Motor Response

Give the student a copy of page 71. Present the following directions.

Look at Row 1.

- Look at the letter *B*. Then, cross out the fourth letter after that *B* and be sure to use a black marker.
- If the letter *G* is the seventh letter of the alphabet, then write a number *7* above it. Decide which letter is the third letter of the alphabet and write a number *3* above that letter.
- Use four of the letters to make the word for the part of your body that has ears, eyes, nose, mouth, and hair. Write that word under the letters, using a blue pen.

Look at Row 2.

- Draw a short, horizontal line to the left of the *16*. Write the number that comes before *16* on that line. Then, draw a short, horizontal line to the right of the *16*.
- Write the number that comes after *16* on the short, horizontal line to the right of the *6*. Cross out the number *3* in *32* and write the number *7* in its place.
- Draw a diagonal line to the left of the *72*. Write the number that comes before it on the diagonal line. Finally, draw a green rectangle around these two numbers.

Look at Row 3.

- With the red marker, write the number of corners for the diamond. With the green marker, write the number of corners for the square. Be sure to write the numbers in the middle of each shape.
- With the blue marker, draw a small arrow pointing toward each corner of the triangle. Write the number of arrows in the middle of that shape. Then, draw a purple circle around that shape.
- Using the purple marker, make a large dot in each corner of the hexagon. Write the number of dots in the center of that shape. Then, use a blackmarker to cross out each dot.

Following Directions

Listen carefully to the directions for each row.

Row 1

A B C D E F G H

Row 2

32   16

Row 3

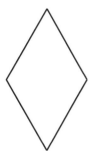  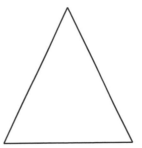 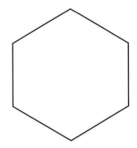

Gross-Motor Response

Materials: none

1. Tell me something on the floor that's not a chair. Then, tell me something on the wall that's not a light switch. Finally, tell me something on the floor that's not the carpet.

2. First, jump up. Then, raise your hands in the air to try and touch the ceiling. Finally, do six jumping jacks.

3. Describe something in this room that's made of wood. Don't tell me what it is unless I ask you to. Let me guess after your second clue.

Fine-Motor Response

Give the student a copy of page 74. Present the following directions.

Look at Row 1.

• In the upper-left corner of the first square, write a question mark. Then, in the lower-right corner of the same square, write a period. Then, draw a dotted, diagonal line from the upper-right corner of that square to the lower-left corner.

• Draw a purple, dotted line from the upper-left corner of the second square to the lower-left corner of the third square. Then, add an arrow on each end of the dotted line.

• Write the number that follows 2 in the middle square and the number that comes before 9 in the last square. Then, connect the two numbers with a large, blue oval.

Look at Row 2.

• Before you write the number 3 in the second circle, write the number 9 in the fourth circle. Then, make a check mark above the circle that has the largest number.

• After you outline the first circle with your yellow marker, write the sum of 10 + 6 in that circle. Then, write that number again under the third circle.

• With your purple marker, draw a dotted line from the circle with the smallest number to the circle with the largest number. Then, take one away from 16 and write that number in the last circle. Be sure to use a black pen.

Following Directions

Name _____

Listen carefully to the directions for each row.

Row 1

Row 2

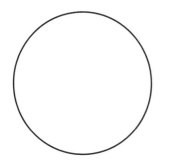 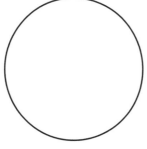  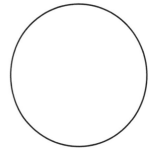

Gross-Motor Response

Materials: scarf, something metal

1. Tell me the name of your favorite dinner food. Then, describe what it tastes like and how it is made.

2. Pretend to play the piano while standing up. Be sure to turn at least two pages. Don't look at your fingers, but rather at the ceiling.

3. Cover your eyes with this scarf first. I'll make a sound using something that's metal in this room. After three seconds, you guess what it is.

Fine-Motor Response

Give the student a copy of page 75. Present the following directions.

Look at Row 1.

* Draw a circle around the number that is the sum of $9 + 9$. Cross out the odd number and write an even number next to it.

* Draw a diagonal line to the right of the number *22*. Write the number that follows it below the diagonal line. Then, draw an arrow pointing up next to the new number.

* Draw a diagonal line to the left of the number *18*. Write the number that comes before it on the diagonal line. Then, draw an arrow pointing down next to the new number.

Look at Row 2.

* Using a short, horizontal line, underline the letter that comes after *L*. Then, draw another short, horizontal line above the same letter. Finally, use a diamond to surround everything you just did.

* Think of the letter the word *rabbit* begins with. Cross out that letter and write the last letter from the word *rabbit* underneath the letter you crossed out.

* When spelling the word *zebra*, you need two of the letters in this set. Write number *1* above the letter that comes first and write a number *2* above the letter that comes second. Use your yellow marker to highlight each letter.

Following Directions

Listen carefully to the directions for each row.

Row 1

18   22   36   11

Row 2

B   R   M   Z

Gross-Motor Response

Materials: new tape roll, yellow highlighter, gold envelope, chapter book

1. Bring me a new roll of tape from the table, the yellow highlighter that's behind the book, and the large gold envelope from under my chair.

2. Think of a letter between *S* and *Z*. Write it on my left shoulder with your pointer finger and tell me to guess what you wrote after four seconds.

3. Open the book to the table of contents. Then, turn to the first page of chapter two and show me the index.

Fine-Motor Response

Give the student a copy of page 77. Present the following directions.

Look at Row 1.

• Draw a solid, blue line from the handle of the mop to the bristles of the broom, going below the bucket and above the shovel. Then, draw a red arrow pointing toward the bucket.

• Write the letter *S* in the blade of the shovel. Then, draw a small box and tie it to the handle of the shovel.

• Write the letter *P* in the small box. Draw a small puddle of water below the mop and draw a small mound of dirt to the left of the shovel.

Look at Row 2.

• Between the triangle and the circle, write a plus sign. Then, write an equal sign between the circle and the diamond after you write the number *14* in the triangle.

• Before you write another number, get a blue pen. Then, write the number that comes before *6* in the circle and the number that comes after *18* in the diamond.

• Draw a vertical line to the right of the diamond. Then, make another diamond and divide it in half, using a horizontal line.

Following Directions

Name _____

Listen carefully to the directions for each row.

Row 1

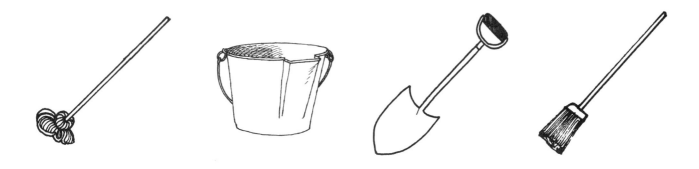

Row 2

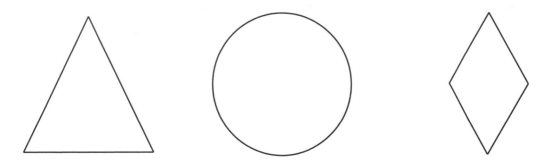

Gross-Motor Response

Materials: tape, paper, large envelope, small envelope

1. First, blink your eyes twice. Second, pat your cheeks three times. Third, touch both of your shoulders, left side first.

2. First, name a red flower. Second, name a toy for babies. Finally, name your favorite school subject from last year.

3. Fold a piece of paper in half and put it in the smaller envelope. Then, seal it with a piece of tape.

Fine-Motor Response

Give the student a copy of page 79. Present the following directions.

Look at Row 1.

*   Draw two short, horizontal lines to the left of the letter *C*. Then, write the first two letters of the alphabet on these lines. Be sure to use uppercase letters.

*   Draw one short, horizontal line to the left of the letter *K* and one short, horizontal line to the right of the letter *K*. Finally, write in the letters that come before and after *K* on the lines you added. Be sure to use lowercase letters.

*   Write the word that means the opposite of *in*, using the last letter of the set to begin. Be sure to use uppercase letters.

Look at Row 2.

*   Cross out the flag on the boat, using a red marker. Color the hull of the boat blue and add a large sail.

*   Draw a small pet door at the bottom of the big door. Make the doorknob larger. Make smoke come out of the train's smoke stack and draw a circle around the engine.

*   Before you draw a fish between the boat and the door, draw a small section of railroad track in front of the train. Then, draw a big rock below the track.

Following Directions

Listen carefully to the directions for each row.

Row 1

C   G   K   O

Row 2

 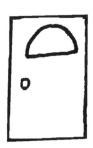 

Gross-Motor Response

Materials: box of crayons, pencil, envelope, chalkboard, chalk, calendar, paper clips

1. Pretend to draw a big circle in the air with the red crayon. Then, draw a large circle in the air with a yellow crayon. Finally, select the crayon that shows what color you make when you mix red and yellow.

2. Spell the color of the pencil. Then, put a paper clip on the calendar and an envelope under the box of crayons.

3. Walk to the chalkboard. Write today's date with chalk. Then, say the date aloud with a loud voice.

Fine-Motor Response

Give the student a copy of page 81. Present the following directions.

Look at Row 1.

- Cross out the vowels in the first word. Then, circle the word that represents a body part needed to hear, and make a check mark on the last letter of the fourth word.

- Write the initial consonant of the third word above that word. Then, draw a line under the word that begins with a blend and draw a diamond shape around the word that rhymes with the first word.

- Think of a word that rhymes with *run* and write it below that word. Then, write the name of a body part that begins with *E* that isn't *ear*. Write it below the word *ear*.

Look at Row 2.

- Draw a zigzag line above the word that is the opposite of *night*. Then, draw a dotted line above the word that means almost the same thing as *happy*. Be sure to use a blue crayon for both lines.

- Each time you see the first letter of the alphabet, make a check mark on it. Then, write the number that tells you how many times you saw that letter to the right of the word *glad*. Be sure to use a red crayon.

- Draw a circle around the word that means the opposite of *little*. Then, write the first letters of the words *large* and *huge* outside of the circle, using an orange marker and uppercase letters.

Following Directions

Name _____

Listen carefully to the directions for each row.

Row 1

look   ear   run   stop   book

Row 2

big   day   glad

Gross-Motor Response

Materials: none

1. Stretch your arms up toward the ceiling. Then, stretch your arms down toward the floor and take a deep breath through your nose.

2. Write the name of a toy on my back with your thumb. The word should begin with an *S* and have at least five letters.

3. Tell me the name of your favorite hard candy. Describe what it looks like, beginning with the paper wrapper, and then describe its taste, being sure to use the word *sweet*.

Fine-Motor Response

Give the student a copy of page 83. Present the following directions.

Look at Row 1.

*   Using markers, color the apple red, the leaves of the apple green, and the stem of the apple brown.

*   Color three seeds of the watermelon black and four seeds brown. Then, color the rind of the watermelon green.

*   Color the banana yellow. Then, write a capital *Y* to the left of the banana and a lowercase *B* to the right of the banana.

Look at Row 2.

*   Color the thing that is used to hit a ball brown. Outline the ball with a black marker and draw a blue line under it.

*   Think of a word that rhymes with *hat* and write it to the right of the cap, but be sure to draw a vertical line next to the cap first.

*   Draw four balls in four different positions around the chair, being sure not to forget the positions of *under, in back of,* and *in front of*. Color the balls four different colors.

Following Directions

Name _____

Listen carefully to the directions for each row.

Row 1

  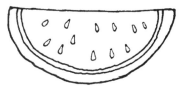

Row 2

Gross-Motor Response

Materials: paper, pencil

1. Turn off the overhead light in this room. Then, tell me if there's anything you can't see clearly. Then, turn that light back on.

2. Pretend to be a baby; drink your bottle holding it with one hand, and then crawl on the floor until you reach the door.

3. Think of something in a garden that is red. Draw it in the upper-left corner of a piece of paper and whisper what it is in my right ear.

Fine-Motor Response

Give the student a copy of page 85. Present the following directions.

Look at Row 1.

*   Write the first letter of the word *book* in the first triangle. Write the first letter of the word *ear* in the second triangle. Be sure you use the lowercase form.

*   Write the second letter of the word *cat* in the third triangle and the third letter of the word *cart* in the last triangle. Be sure to use a red pencil.

*   Draw a simple picture of the thing this word spells. Be sure to use a brown crayon and position the picture below the triangles.

Look at Row 2.

*   Make a check mark over the smallest square. Then, draw a line under the square that is a little larger and a line above the square that is still larger, but not the largest.

*   Draw a big, blue circle around the largest square and a small, green circle in the middle of that square. Then, make a red dot in the middle of that small circle.

*   Draw a wavy, yellow line from the lower-left corner of the first square to the upper-right corner of the last square, going above the second square and through the third square. Be sure to go through the small circle that's inside the largest square.

Following Directions

Name _____

Listen carefully to the directions for each row.

Row 1

Row 2

Maintaining Conversations . . . .

The purpose of teaching your students to maintain a conversation within an environment of background noise is to generalize their improved auditory processing to a more naturalistic context.

With your student, decide on topics for maintaining five-minute conversations, both within the therapy session and for home practice. Again, use the progression below for background noise, implementing weekly progressions to the next level. Once the student can maintain a conversation at the *television* level, proceed to the next section, *Completing Seatwork*.

Progression for Background Noise

low-level, continuous	appliances, such as a fan, a clothes dryer, or a dishwasher
non-specific music	a radio or CD featuring music that the student finds very uninteresting/nondistracting; volume low, yet distinctive
specific music	a radio or CD featuring music that the student finds very appealing/distracting
radio talk shows	initially presented with low, yet distinctive, volume; later presented with varying volume levels to better mirror the varied volume levels found within most classrooms
television	The student sits with his/her back towards the TV; a program of no interest to the student is featured. Once the student masters this level, feature programs of great interest and use a remote control to vary volume levels.

Completing Seatwork . . . .

This section involves completing seatwork in an environment of background noise. The actual work is usually completed as a home activity.

The student begins with five-minute increments of homework at the *low-level, continuous noise* level. As the student maintains comfort at this level, increase the time increments up to twenty-minute segments.

Use the same progression through the background noise hierarchy as above, although the changes within the hierarchy are more fluid and variable at this point. Some students may move upward twice within a week; others may need to stay at one noise level for several weeks until they feel comfortable for twenty working minutes.

Following Lectures　.　.　.　.　.　.　.　.　.　.　.　.　.　.　.

This section provides typical classroom lecture segments. Read an appropriate level to a student, using talk radio or TV with varying intensity levels for background noise. The student then evidences comprehension of and retention for the material by emphasizing the most important information when paraphrasing it back to you. A checklist is provided with each lecture for your convenience in determining if the student has met this objective.

Grade Level	Lecture Title	Page
2	Germs	88
2	Dinosaurs	89
3	Teeth	90
3	The Moon	91
4	Bees	92
4	The Respiratory System	93
5	Magnets	94
5	Stars	95
6	The Atom	96
6	Metals	97
7	The Elements of Survival	98
7	A Strange Fungus	99
8	The Water Cycle	100
8	Earth's Landscapes	101

Following Lectures

Germs

Since germs cannot be seen, we may think they do not exist. We may also think that there is nothing we can do to help spread germs or to help stop germs from spreading. Well, these ideas are all wrong! Germs are very real and we can do a lot to help spread or stop them. One of the most important things that we can do to stop germs from spreading is to wash our hands. We should wash our hands after using the bathroom. We should wash our hands before we eat. Using disinfectants is another good way to stop germs in their tracks. Anti-bacterial soaps help prevent the spread of germs on your skin. Alcohol and bleach help prevent the spread of germs in our environment. Did you know that antibiotics are disinfectants, too? They destroy germs that are in your body.

Check whether or not the student remembered these ideas in paraphrasing the above information.

	yes	no
1. Germs can be spread from person to person and from place to place.		
2. We should wash our hands before eating and after using the bathroom.		
3. Disinfectants help to destroy germs.		
4. Soap, alcohol, and bleach are examples of disinfectants for the outside of the body.		
5. Antibiotics are disinfectants for the inside of the body.		

Following Lectures

Name _____

Dinosaurs

Dinosaurs—the "terrible lizards." Scientists now believe that birds, not lizards, are the descendants of the dinosaurs. Some dinosaurs were cold-blooded animals. Can you think of some cold-blooded animals that live on Earth today? If you thought of snakes, frogs, or crocodiles, then you did some good thinking! Some dinosaurs were warm-blooded animals. Examples of warm-blooded animals that live on Earth today include cows, horses, and people. Although dinosaurs lived many millions of years before any human inhabited Earth, we have learned a lot about these creatures. By finding fossilized footprints and bones, we know what they looked like. The library has many nonfiction books that explain dinosaur habits and many fiction books that make for reading fun.

Check whether or not the student remembered these ideas in paraphrasing the above information.

	yes	no
1. The word *dinosaur* means "terrible lizard."		
2. Dinosaurs are the ancestors of birds.		
3. Some dinosaurs were cold-blooded, like today's snakes.		
4. Some dinosaurs were warm-blooded, like today's horses.		
5. Fossils help us to learn about dinosaurs.		

Following Lectures

Name _____

Teeth

The next time that you take a bite out of a delicious, juicy, crisp apple, think about how difficult it would be to enjoy this food without teeth! Teeth allow us to eat all kinds of foods that help keep us healthy and help us to grow strong. Because our teeth are so important to our overall good health, it's very important to keep our teeth healthy as well. We keep our teeth healthy when we brush them thoroughly and floss them carefully. Regular visits to the dentist also help to keep teeth healthy. Unhealthy teeth are surrounded by lots of bacteria. The bacteria coats the teeth with a substance called *plaque*, which can cause gum disease. The bacteria also forms an acid that eats through teeth and can form caries, or cavities.

Check whether or not the student remembered these ideas in paraphrasing the above information

	yes	no
1. Teeth allow us to eat all kinds of foods.		
2. We keep teeth healthy by brushing and flossing.		
3. We should see a dentist regularly.		
4. Plaque can cause gum disease.		
5. Bacteria can form acid that eats into teeth.		

Following Lectures

The Moon

If you look up at the sky the next time there is a full moon, you might think that you can see a smiling face looking back at you! Over the years, there have been many stories told about the moon, ranging from nursery rhymes to books and even movies. Unlike its appearance, the moon is a cold, dark mass of rock about four times smaller than our Earth. It is covered with mountains, hills, and large plains that resemble seas when you look through a telescope. The moon is also covered with many bowl-shaped pits called *craters*. Scientists think these craters were formed when chunks of rock fell on the surface of the moon from outer space. Once these chunks of rock fall on to a surface, such as the moon, they are called *meteorites*.

Check whether or not the student remembered these ideas in paraphrasing the above information

	yes	no
1. The moon is four times smaller than the Earth.		
2. The moon has mountains, hills, and plains.		
3. The moon is covered with craters.		
4. Craters are bowl-shaped pits.		
5. Rocks that fall from space to the ground are called *meteorites*.		

Following Lectures

Name _____

Bees

"Look at the people dancing!" When someone says this to you, it brings forth images of people at parties, listening to good music and having fun. So what do you think about when someone says, "Look at the bees dancing"? That's right—bees also dance, but they dance for a different reason. Worker bees dance to let other worker bees know where to go to get food. Food for bees is a sweet liquid called *nectar* that bees gather from flowers. When a worker bee does the round dance, it is telling its hive mates that nectar is nearby. When the worker bee does the wagging dance at an angle, it is telling its hive mates to follow that angle, either towards the sun or away from the sun, to get to the nectar. A slow wagging dance indicates the nectar is farther away and a fast wagging dance indicates the necter is closer to the hive at the particular angle indicated.

Check whether or not the student remembered these ideas in paraphrasing the above information.

	yes	no
1. Bees dance to tell other bees how to get to the food.		
2. Nectar is a sweet liquid that is found in flowers.		
3. When flowers are nearby, bees do the round dance.		
4. Bees do the wagging dance at an angle, either toward the sun or away from the sun.		
5. When flowers are farther away, bees do a fast wagging dance.		

Following Lectures

Name _____

The Respiratory System

Your body has special parts that are used for breathing. Breathing is what you do when you bring air into your body and then push it out of your body. The parts of your body that are used for breathing make up the respiratory system and consist of the nose, mouth, windpipe, lungs, and diaphragm. When you inhale, or take air into your body through your nose, the air is cleaned, warmed, and moistened by the small hairs that grow in your nose. The air from your nose or mouth is pushed into your windpipe, which connects to your lungs. Your lungs are two spongy bags that get bigger when you inhale and get smaller when you push the air out of your body for the exhale. All of this pushing is made possible by the diaphragm. The diaphragm is a muscle that pushes downward to give your lungs more room to fill up on the inhale and then pushes upward to help squeeze the air out of your lungs for the exhale.

Check whether or not the student remembered these ideas in paraphrasing the above information.

	yes	no
1. The respiratory system consists of the mouth, nose, windpipe, lungs, and diaphragm.		
2. The hairs in our noses clean, warm, and moisten the air we inhale.		
3. The windpipe connects the nose and mouth to the lungs.		
4. Our lungs get bigger and smaller as we inhale and exhale.		
5. The diaphragm pushes down or up to help the lungs inhale or exhale.		

Following Lectures

Name _____

Magnets

"Oh, no—the box of paper clips fell on the floor. What a mess!" Do you want a quick way to pick them up? Well, just grab a magnet, pull it over the paper clips, and you'll have that mess cleaned up quickly. What are magnets? Simply stated, a magnet is a metal object that attracts other metal objects. Iron and steel are the best metals to use for magnets. Magnets can be found in many places within our homes. They are the part of the electric can opener that lifts the lid. They are the part of the note or picture hanger that sticks on the refrigerator. When you put two magnets near each other on a table, you may notice that they pull towards each other some of the time and move farther apart at other times. Magnets have poles. When the north pole of one magnet faces the north pole of another magnet, they move farther apart. This principal holds true for the south poles, also. But when the north pole of one magnet faces the south pole of another magnet, they pull toward each other.

Check whether or not the student remembered these ideas in paraphrasing the above information.

	yes	no
1. A magnet is a metal object that attracts other metal objects.		
2. Iron and steel make the best magnets.		
3. Can openers and refrigerator picture holders contain magnets.		
4. Like poles (north and north or south and south) facing each other cause magnets to move farther apart.		
5. Opposite poles (north and south) facing each other cause magnets to move closer together.		

Following Lectures

Name _____

Stars

When you look at a star, you might think of making a wish. When a scientist looks at a star, she is probably thinking of how to classify it. Stars are classified by brightness, size, temperature, and color. When stars shine with a bluish light, they are very hot stars, averaging 11,000 degrees Celsius or higher. When stars shine with a reddish light, they are cooler stars averaging 3,500 degrees Celsius or less. From this information, you can see that a star's color is related to its temperature. Stars come in all different sizes with no relation to temperature, color, or brightness. Stars also have varying degrees of brightness, again with no relation to temperature, color, or size. Stars do have one factor in common. They are balls of hot gases that produce vast quantities of energy. Now that you know so much about stars, how would you classify our sun? Scientists would agree with you if you said that our sun is a yellow star of average size with a relatively cooler temperature, 5,000 to 6,000 degrees Celsius.

Check whether or not the student remembered these ideas in paraphrasing the above information.

	yes	no
1. Stars are classified by brightness, size, temperature, and color.		
2. Hot stars are bluish and are 11,000 degrees Celcius or hotter.		
3. Cool stars are reddish and are 3,500 degrees Celsius or cooler.		
4. All stars produce energy.		
5. Our sun is average sized, yellow, and on the cooler side (5,000 to 6,000 degrees Celsius).		

Following Lectures

Name _____

The Atom

Do you remember opening a box full of Lego® blocks and sorting them so you could build your newest model? Each piece had its own important place in creating a strong, functional product. When scientists work with atoms, it's like when you work with Lego® blocks. Each atom has an important place in creating a piece of matter. In fact, atoms are referred to as the "building blocks of matter." Unlike Lego® blocks, however, atoms are very complex little blocks. They consist of a nucleus containing the subatomic particles called *protons* and *neutrons*. The word *subatomic* means that these particles are smaller than the atom itself. The particles of proton have a positive charge, while the particles of neutron are neutral, meaning that they have no charge. Circling around the nucleus is the third kind of subatomic particle called *electrons*. These particles have a negative charge.

Check whether or not the student remembered these ideas in paraphrasing the above information.

	yes	no
1. Atoms are called the "building blocks of matter."		
2. Atoms have a center called a *nucleus*.		
3. *Subatomic* means "smaller than an atom."		
4. Protons and neutrons are subatomic particles located within the nucleus.		
5. Electrons are subatomic particles located all around a nucleus.		

Following Lectures

Name _____

Metals

When a scientist classifies a particular piece of matter as a metal, he or she has gone through a checklist of primarily physical properties to help in making that decision. The six physical properties make metal fairly easy to identify. *Luster* means that metal is shiny—think of a new penny. *Ductile* means that metal can be drawn out into strings—think of thin wires. *Malleable* means that metal can be hammered into thin sheets—think of aluminum foil. *Conduction* means that heat and electricity move through metal easily—think of an electric stove. *Density* means that metals are heavy in relation to their size—think of weights. *Melting point* means that metals will become liquid at high temperatures—think about molten steel. Using this checklist, you will find that most of the matter on Earth is classified as a metal.

Check whether or not the student remembered these ideas in paraphrasing the above information.

	yes	no
1. Metals are classified according to six physical properties.		
2. Most matter on Earth is metal.		
Use this guide to score items 3-5 below. Give the student full credit for listing 3 of the 6 physical properties by name, accompanied by an explanation (i.e., "*Luster* means shiny, *ductile* means draw out into thin strings," etc.). Give the student half credits for listing a term or its explanation only.		
3.		
4.		
5.		

Following Lectures

The Elements of Survival

"If you're alive, you want to survive!" Whether you say that as part of a rap tune or say it as part of a serious lecture, it is true however you say it. Every living organism has basic needs to ensure its survival. Energy is one need. Without energy, animals couldn't hunt for food. Without energy, people couldn't plant crops. All energy comes from the sun, including the plants that change light into food and the animals that eat the plants. All living things need food and water. Food not only supplies energy but also provides the nutrients necessary for growth and repair of cells. Water is the major component of organisms and allows for nutrients to circulate around the organism and for waste to be carried away. Without oxygen, no living organism could survive. Some organisms get oxygen from the air, as with mammals, and others get oxygen from the water, as with marine life. All living organisms compete for enough space in which to live. Finally, an organism must maintain proper body temperature in order to survive. The next time you begin complaining about excessive perspiration, stop to think. Without all that water running off of your body, your temperature would escalate and you wouldn't be a survivor!

Check whether or not the student remembered these ideas in paraphrasing the above information.

	yes	no
1. Survival requires energy; the ultimate source is the sun.		
2. Survival requires food and water. Food supplies energy; water is the major component of living organisms.		
3. Survival requires oxygen.		
4. Survival requires enough space in which to live and satisfy basic needs.		
5. Survival requires appropriate body temperatures for particular organisms.		

Following Lectures

Name _____

A Strange Fungus

The next time you lick your lips at the thought of eating a slice of pizza with all the toppings, including mushrooms; or some delectable, stuffed mushroom caps; or a thick steak covered with sauteed mushrooms, remember one thing—a mushroom is a fungus. A fungus is classified as a heterotroph, meaning that it cannot make its own food but relies on a host to obtain its food.

The mushroom has many relatives, including one that kills ants! This fungus looks like a bit of dust as it lands on the back of an ant. Almost immediately upon landing, tiny tentacles emerge from the speck and start to grow into the ant's body. The tentacles release chemicals that dissolve the ant's tissues, turning it into food for the fungus. The tentacles grow rapidly throughout the ant's body and, within a few days, only a hollow shell is left. At this point, the tentacles grow out of the shell and merge into a long stalk to produce a spore pod. The wind carries these spores to new victims.

Check whether or not the student remembered these ideas in paraphrasing the above information.

	yes	no
1. A mushroom is a fungus.		
2. A fungus is a heterotroph.		
3. A heterotroph doesn't produce its own food. It relies on a host for its food.		
4. One kind of fungus kills ants.		
5. The ant-killing fungus uses its tentacles to dissolve the ant's tissues, leaving only a hollow shell.		

Following Lectures

Name _____

The Water Cycle

The water cycle consists of three steps—evaporation, condensation, and precipitation. Because of this cycle, the earth maintains a consistently renewed supply of fresh water. The process called evaporation is driven by heat from the sun, which causes water to change into water vapor. Water evaporates from saltwater sources, such as oceans, from freshwater sources, such as lakes and rivers, and from the soil itself. Plants and animals release water vapor directly. As water evaporates, it leaves all trace minerals behind, including salt. Therefore, all water vapor is fresh water. The process called condensation involves the cooling of the water vapor, causing it to condense or form into water droplets. Because this usually happens high above the earth, the droplets gather together as clouds. When these clouds become too heavy and full of water droplets, the process called precipitation occurs. The droplets fall back to the earth in the form of rain, hail, sleet, or snow, depending on the temperature of the air. The cycle is now complete and ready for the evaporation phase once again.

Check whether or not the student remembered these ideas in paraphrasing the above information.

	yes	no
1. The water cycle provides the earth with a constant supply of fresh water.		
2. Evaporation is the first part of the cycle and results from water being heated by the sun and turned into vapor.		
3. All water vapor is fresh water, regardless of its source.		
4. Condensation is the second part of the cycle and results from the vapor being cooled back into water droplets.		
5. Precipitation, the third part of the cycle, results from heavy clouds that release water in the form of rain, snow, sleet, or hail, depending on the temperature.		

Following Lectures

Earth's Landscapes

Earth's landscape is characterized primarily by regions of mountains, plains, and plateaus. These regions are understood and defined by their elevation levels. A mountainous landscape consists of narrow tops called *summits*, steep sides, and elevation levels referenced to the level of the sea. For example, Pike's Peak in Colorado is approximately 4,300 meters above sea level. A landscape consisting of plains is relatively flat and relatively close to sea level. Rivers and streams abound and grassy-type plants thrive in this region. Some plains are close to the oceans and thus are called *coastal plains*. Other plains are found in the interior portion of a continent and thus are called *interior plains*. A landscape consisting of plateaus is relatively flat, but is found at higher elevation levels than plains. Most plateaus are located within the interior portion of a continent. A few plateaus, however, are near oceans and are recognized as cliffs.

Check whether or not the student remembered these ideas in paraphrasing the above information.

	yes	no
1. Elevation levels help to define Earth's surfaces.		
2. Elevation is referenced to the level of the sea.		
3. Mountains have the highest elevation and are recognized by steep sides and narrow summits.		
4. Plains are flat areas that are very close to sea level.		
5. Plateaus are flat areas and have a much higher elevation than plains.		

Auditory Cohesion

Auditory cohesion involves higher-level linguistic processing skills. A deficit in this area may affect students' abilities to follow directions correctly in school or at home, take notes, and to express themselves in writing. Helping students to identify key words in messages is one way to improve their linguistic processing skills and their abilities to follow directions correctly.

Understanding Key Words from Directions

Before presenting these items, copy the appropriate word card pages (see pages 108 to 118) and cut the cards apart.

Present each direction aloud. After you finish, have the student tell you the key words necessary to complete the directions you just gave. As the student identifies these key words, hand the corresponding word card to the student to help her keep in mind the targets she has achieved. Prompt the student to elicit any remaining key words.

Grade Level 2

1. You are going to see the beginning of a web about helping others. Brainstorm different ways to help people. Then, write the ideas in the appropriate places on the web with your pencil. (list on page 108)

2. I'm going to read some sentences of realistic fiction and nonrealistic fiction. Realistic fiction has characters that act like real people, animals that act like real animals, and a plot that could really happen in a setting that could be real. As you listen to these sentences, decide if they belong in realistic fiction or nonrealistic fiction. (list on page 108)

3. You are going to read sentences that have a missing word. Then, you're going to read a pair of words that could be used to fill in the blank space. You will decide which word best completes the sentence and circle that word. (list on page 108)

4. We're going to play a word game. You will choose one three-letter blend from Column A and try to make as many words as you can, using the letter groups from Column B. The person who makes the most correct words will be the winner. (list on page 108)

5. I'm going to describe how to put together a terrarium. To refresh your memory, a terrarium is a closed container where plants and animals can live together. When I'm finished talking, you will read some sentences and number them for the correct order that I described. (list on page 109)

Grade Level 3

1. I want you to review the story of *The Three Little Pigs*. Then, you are going to create a web for some of the different important words from the story. Feel free to use other words, phrases, or images for the target words. (list on page 109)

2. The phonogram *ost* has the same sound as the short vowel *O*. As you look at the words below, I want you to circle the phonogram or short vowel sound in each. Then, I want you to use those same words to complete the sentences. (list on page 109)

3. The setting of a story is when it takes place and/or where it takes place. Some things can happen in one setting but are impossible to happen in another. Cut apart the sentences below. Put all the sentences that have a setting that could really happen in one pile. Put all the sentences that have a setting that could never really happen in another pile. (list on page 109)

4. Sometimes, you can look at each part of a compound word and it will help you to know what the word means. Sometimes, the word will remind you of another compound word that is similar in meaning. First, draw a line from the words in Column A to the words in Column B that best go together. Then, using your red marker, divide each compound word so that each part stands alone. (list on page 110)

5. Read the words below. Decide how you can give each word a shape so that each word's meaning can be understood easily. Then, use the boxes provided to complete your work. The first one is done for you. (list on page 110)

Grade Level 4

1. Today, we're going to practice introductions. We are going to pretend that we don't know each other. We're going to introduce ourselves to each other, remembering to tell something about us to help get us started talking to each other. You will go first. (list on page 110)

2. You are going to read sentences that are written in the present tense. You will need to change each sentence to the past tense. Look at your choices in the box. Cut the words apart and glue them over the appropriate verb in each sentence. (list on pages 110 and 111)

3. The long *A* sound is the same sound made by the phonograms *ail, ain,* and *ay*. I want you to think of two words with each phonogram and two words with the long *A* sound. Next, I want you to write these words on your paper, using a red pen for the phonograms and a black pen for the other letters. (list on page 111)

4. Many times, one word can have two completely different meanings. As I say a word, I want you to draw two pictures to show the two different meanings for that word. Then, I want you to tell me a sentence using both meanings of the word in the same sentence. (list on page 111)

5. I am going to give you a bag containing several objects. You will make a chart on this piece of paper. Divide the paper in half, and for the column on the left, write the object's name. For the column on the right, write a description of the object. First you will observe the objects and describe them. Then, you will handle those same objects and add any new information to your chart. (list on page 111)

Grade Level 5

1. We're going to examine this plant. You are going to tell me all the parts of the plant that you can see and the parts below the soil that you can't see. Then, you're going to examine the leaves. Be sure to tell me how the leaves are attached, how thick they are, and how the width compares to the length. (list on page 112)

2. There are three important things to remember when you summarize something that you have read. Your summary should be short, it should contain important information, and it should relate the information in order. First, I want you to give me a summary of your day. Then, I want you to read this article and summarize it. (list on page 112)

3. I'm going to write several words on this piece of paper. I want you to copy the words on your paper and underline the long vowel in each word with this red pen. Then, I want you to underline the phonograms with the blue pen and read the words aloud. (list on page 113)

4. Prefixes are groups of letters added to the beginnings of words to change their meaning. As you read each word below, highlight the prefix and tell what the word means. Then, think of another word that has almost the same meaning and write it next to the word. (list on page 113)

5. In Column A, you will see words that can be used as the subjects of a sentence. In Column B, you will see words that indicate possession. Draw a line from Column A to Column B to match word pairs. Then, use both words in one sentence. (list on page 113)

Grade Level 6

1. Adverbs help to give detail and exactness to writing. Adverbs are formed by adding -ly to an adjective. Add an adverb to each sentence to tell in what manner the action was performed. Bracket the adjective from which you formed the adverb with your red pen. (list on page 114)

2. Jack London wrote a story called the *King of Mazy May*. The word *Mazy* comes form the word *maze*. Draw a maze on your paper with your red pen. Then, decide how a river could be compared to a maze. Write three main facts pertaining to this idea on the lines below. (list on page 114)

3. A conflict is a struggle between opposing forces. Choose a story that you have read and discuss the conflict incorporating the following elements. (list on page 114)

4. Many words have more than one meaning. For example, if you were to look up the word *saw* in the dictionary, you would see that it has at least two numbered definitions: "a tool for cutting" and "an action performed with your eyes." Look up the meaning of the following words. For each word, write two sentences using a different meaning of the word in each. (list on page 115)

5. Figurative language is used to describe and to make vivid descriptions of people, places, and/or things. After reading the following figurative expressions, name the two things that are being compared. What does each comparison help you to visualize? (list on page 115)

Grade Level 7

1. In order to draw a conclusion, we must have enough facts to help with our thinking. Conclusions can also be called *inferences*. Below, you will read some facts. On the lines below each fact, write a major inference you can draw from the fact. (list on page 115)

2. Many books contain a glossary at the back to explain the way some words are used in that particular book. Using this book (provide a book for the student), find the pronunciation and meaning of three of the words. Then, write your own sentence for each word on the lines below. (list on pages 115 and 116)

3. The following sentences describe different stories that might be written about a character named Mr. Amos. From the list after the sentences, choose the title that best fits each story. Write the letter of the title on the line next to the sentence. (list on page 116)

4. Decide whether the following statements contain realistic or fantastic details. For each statement, write *realistic* or *fantastic* on the line on the right. (list on page 116)

5. Match each word in the left column with its definition in the right column. Write the letter of the definition on the line next to the word it defines. (list on page 116)

1. Compound sentences are sentences that have several closely-related ideas. By combining important ideas, the writer eliminates several choppy sentences. Compound sentences contain commas to separate the independent clauses and a conjunction such as *and, but, for,* or *yet.* As you read the sentences below, substitute a period for the commas and the conjunctions. Then, write two compound sentences of your own. Finally, rewrite your two compound sentences, eliminating the commas and conjunctions to create choppy sentences. (list on page 117)

2. When a word is personified, it is given a human characteristic. Listen to the following sentences as I read them. Decide if the target word has been personified. If yes, explain how it was personified. (list on page 117)

3. Irony is often used in literature. Read the following sentences with accompanying explanations and discuss why irony is part of the format. Then, think of two other sentences or ideas to illustrate irony. (list on pages 117 and 118)

4. Read a passage aloud from a story of your choice. Then, summarize what you have read. Finally, make a prediction about what you think will happen next and silently read a few more paragraphs to see if your prediction was correct. (list on page 118)

5. Below you will find a list of words and a list of definitions. Match the words to the definitions. Then, use the dictionary to confirm or correct your thinking. Finally, write a sentence to illustrate your knowledge for two of the words. (list on page 118)

Central Auditory Processing Kit, Book 3
Auditory Cohesion—Key Words from Directions   107

Understanding Key Words from Directions

Level 2, Item 1

web	helping others
brainstorm	write
pencil	

Level 2, Item 2

realistic fiction	nonrealistic fiction
real people	real animals
real plot	listen
decide	real setting

Level 2, Item 3

read	missing word
pair of words	blank space
decide	circle

Level 2, Item 4

word game	three-letter blend
Column A	many words
letter groups	Column B
most correct words	winner

Understanding Key Words from Directions

Level 2, Item 5

terrarium	container
plants	animals
read sentences	number
correct order	

Level 3, Item 1

review	*The Three Little Pigs*
create	web
important words	phrases
images	target words

Level 3, Item 2

phonogram	short vowel
circle	complete
sentences	same words

Level 3, Item 3

story setting	when it takes place
where it takes place	cut sentences
could really happen	pile
could never really happen	another pile

Understanding Key Words from Directions

Level 3, Item 4

each part	compound word
similar in meaning	draw line
Column A	Column B
red marker	divide
stands alone	what word means

Level 3, Item 5

read	word
shape	meaning
understood	boxes

Level 4, Item 1

introductions	pretend
don't know each other	tell something
started	go first

Level 4, Item 2

read	sentences
present tense	change
past tense	choices

word cards continued on the next page

Understanding Key Words from Directions

Level 4, Item 2 (continued)

box	cut
glue	verb

Level 4, Item 3

long *A*	phonograms
think	two words
each phonogram	write
red pen	black pen
other letters	

Level 4, Item 4

word	different meanings
draw	two pictures
tell	sentence
both meanings	same sentence

Level 4, Item 5

bag	objects
chart	paper
divide in half	left column

word cards continued on the next page

Understanding Key Words from Directions

Level 4, Item 5 *(continued)*

object name	right column
object description	observe
handle	new information

Level 5, Item 1

examine	plant
tell	parts you can see
parts below	examine leaves
how attached	how thick
width	compares to
length	

Level 5, Item 2

three things	remember
summary	short
important information	in order
summary of day	read
article	summarize

Understanding Key Words from Directions

Level 5, Item 3

words	paper
copy	underline
long vowel	red pen
phonograms	blue pen
read aloud	

Level 5, Item 4

prefixes	letters
beginnings	words
change meaning	read
highlight	tell
think	same meaning
write	

Level 5, Item 5

Column A	subjects
one sentence	Column B
possession	draw line
match pairs	both words

Understanding Key Words from Directions

Level 6, Item 1

adverbs	detail
exactness	*-ly*
adjective	add adverb
sentence	tell action
what manner	action performed
bracket adjective	red pen

Level 6, Item 2

Mazy	maze
draw	paper
red pen	river
compared	write
three facts	lines below

Level 6, Item 3

conflict	struggle
opposing forces	story
read	discuss
incorporate	elements

Understanding Key Words from Directions

Level 6, Item 4

more than one meaning	dictionary
definitions	write
two sentences	different meanings

Level 6, Item 5

figurative language	describe
vivid	read
expressions	name
two things	compared
visualize	

Level 7, Item 1

conclusion	facts
thinking	inferences
read	write

Level 7, Item 2

glossary	back of book
explain	words
pronunciation	meaning

word cards continued on the next page

Understanding Key Words from Directions

Level 7, Item 2 *(continued)*

three words	write
sentence	each word

Level 7, Item 3

describe	different stories
character	choose
title	write letter
line next to sentence	Mr. Amos

Level 7, Item 4

realistic	fantastic
details	write
line on right	decide

Level 7, Item 5

match	word
left column	definition
right column	write letter
line next to word	

Understanding Key Words from Directions

Level 8, Item 1

compound sentences	related ideas
combining	eliminate
choppy sentences	commas
separate	independent clauses
conjunction	read sentences
substitute	period
write	two compound sentences
rewrite	create choppy sentences

Level 8, Item 2

personified	human characteristic
listen	sentences
decide	target word
explain	

Level 8, Item 3

irony	read
sentences	explanations
discuss	think

word cards continued on the next page

Understanding Key Words from Directions

Level 8, Item 3 (continued)

two other ideas	illustrate

Level 8, Item 4

read aloud	story
summarize	prediction
silently read	see if correct

Level 8, Item 5

list	words
definitions	match
dictionary	confirm
correct	write
sentence	illustrate knowledge
two words	

Understanding Directions . . . .

In this section, the student will listen to orally-presented directions and then will demonstrate comprehension by performing the directions appropriately. Give the student the appropriate worksheet **after** you have finished giving the directions, unless the directions specify to give the worksheet to the student first.

Grade Level 2

1. Tell the student, "You are going to see the beginning of a web about helping others. Brainstorm different ways to help people. Then, write the ideas in the appropriate places on the web." Give the student a copy of page 126.

2. Tell the student, "I'm going to read some sentences of realistic fiction and nonrealistic fiction. Realistic fiction has characters that act like real people, animals that act like real animals, and a plot that could really happen in a setting that could be real. As you listen to these sentences, tell me if they belong in realistic fiction or nonrealistic fiction."

   As the sun began to set, I felt a little homesick. (realistic)

   John told me that I was his best friend. (realistic)

   Mother pig made a delicious chocolate cake for her baby. (nonrealistic)

   The pony ran fast and jumped over the stream. (realistic)

   The girl jumped into the water, wiggled her nose, and immediately turned into a mermaid. (nonrealistic)

   They flew their plane to the sun because they wanted to get a good tan! (nonrealistic)

3. Tell the student, "You are going to read sentences that have a missing word. Then, you're going to read a pair of words that could be used to fill in the blank space. You will decide which word best completes the sentence and then, circle that word." Give the student a copy of page 127. (Answers: early, field, pulled, sure, believe)

4. Tell the student, "We're going to play a word game. You will choose one three-letter blend from Box A. Each of us will try to make as many words as we can using the letter groups from Box B. The person who makes the most correct words will be the winner." Give the student a copy of page 127 and use another copy for yourself. (Answers: screen, scrawl, scrap, scream, spleen, splay, splint, strung, stray, strain, string, strap, stream, sprung, spray, sprint, sprawl, sprain, spring)

5. Tell the student, "I'm going to describe how to put together a terrarium. A terrarium is a closed container where plants and animals can live together. When I'm finished talking, you will read some sentences and number them for the correct order that I described.

"I'm using a fish aquarium. I put gravel in the bottom and then a thin layer of dirt. I wet the soil slightly and then put a small plant in each corner. I put a slug on one plant, a snail on another plant, and a cricket in the center of the bowl. I add three slices of apple for the cricket to eat. Then, I cover the aquarium with a piece of screen." Give the student a copy of page 128. (Answers: 3, 4, 2, 5, 1)

Grade Level 3

1. Tell the student, "I want you to review the story of *The Three Little Pigs.* Then, you are going to create a web for some of the different important words from the story. Feel free to use other words, phrases or images for the target words." Either provide a copy of the book *The Three Little Pigs* or tell the story. Then, give the student a copy of page 129.

2. Give the student a copy of page 130. Say, "As you look at the words on this list, I want you to circle the phonogram or vowel sound in each word. Then, use those same words to complete the sentences." (Answers: 1. lost, 2. cost, 3. Boston, 4. frost)

3. Give the student a copy of page 130. Say, "The setting of a story is when it takes place and/or where it takes place. Some things can happen in one setting but are impossible to happen in another.

"Cut apart the sentences on this page. Put all the sentences that have a setting that could really happen in one pile. Put all the sentences that have a setting that could never really happen in another pile." (Answers: *a, c,* and *d* couldn't really happen; b, e, and *f* could really happen)

4. Give the student a copy of page 131. Say, "Sometimes, you can look at each part of a compound word and it will help you to know what the word means. Sometimes, the word will remind you of another compound word that is similar in meaning.

"First, draw a line from the words in Column A to the words in Column B that best go together. Then, using your red marker, divide each compound word so that each part stands alone." (Answers: air•port/ air•line, water•front/water•melon, head•line/under•line, news•paper/ news•print, screw•ball/screw•driver)

5. Give the student a copy of page 132. Say, "Read the words on this page. Decide how you can give each word a shape so that the meaning of the word can be understood easily. Then, use the boxes provided to complete your work. The first one is done for you." (Answers will vary.)

Grade Level 4

1. Tell the student, "Today, we're going to practice introductions. We are going to pretend that we don't know each other. We're going to introduce ourselves to each other, remembering to tell something about us to help get us started talking to each other. You will go first."

2. Give the student a copy of page 133. Say, "You are going to read sentences that are written in the present tense. You will need to change each sentence to the past tense.

   "Look at your choices in the box. Cut the words apart and glue them over the appropriate verb in each sentence." (Answers: a. was, b. rode, c. ate, d. were, e. wrote, f. shook)

3. Give the student a copy of page 133. Say, "The long *A* sound is the same sound made by the phonograms *ail, ain,* and *ay.*

   "I want you to think of two words with each phonogram and two words with the long *A* sound. Next, I want you to write these words on your paper, using a red pen for the phonograms and a black pen for the other letters." (Answers will vary.)

4. Give the student a copy of page 134. Say, "Many times, one word can have two completely different meanings. As I say a word, I want you to draw two pictures to show the two different meanings for that word. Then, I want you to tell me a sentence using both meanings of the word in the same sentence." (possible meanings below)

   saw   a. past tense of *see*
              b. tool to cut wood/to cut something with a saw

   glasses   a. lenses in a frame to help you see better
              b. things you drink from

   bark   a. skin or covering of a tree
              b. sound a dog makes/to make noise

   rock   a. large stone
              b. to move back and forth, as in a rocking chair

   pit   a. fruit stone or seed
              b. deep opening or hole

5. Gather these objects and put them in a bag: feather, rock, piece of bark, toothpick, cotton ball.

   Give the student a piece of paper. Say, "I am going to give you a bag containing several objects. You will make a chart on this piece of paper. Divide the paper in half. In the column on the left, write each object's name. For the column on the right, write a description of each object. First, you will observe the objects and describe them. Then, you will handle those same objects and add any new information to your chart." (Answers will vary.)

Grade Level 5

1. Have a plant available. Tell the student, "You are going to tell me all the parts of this plant that you can see and the parts that are below the soil that you can't see. Then, you're going to examine the leaves and describe them to me. Be sure to tell me how the leaves are attached, how thick they are, and how their width compares to their length. (Answers will vary.)

2. Have a magazine or newspaper article available. Tell the student, "There are three important things to remember when you summarize something that you have read. Your summary should be short, it should contain important information, and it should relate the information in order.

   "First I want you to give me a summary of your day. Then, I want you to read this article and summarize it."

3. Have a red pen, a blue pen, and two sheets of paper available. Tell the student, "I'm going to write several words on this piece of paper. I want you to copy the words on your paper and underline the long vowel in each word with this red pen. Then, I want you to underline the phonograms with the blue pen and read the words aloud."

   Write these words on your paper: might, assignment, like, flashlight, write, sign. Give your paper to the student to copy.

4. Give the student a copy of page 135. Say, "Prefixes are groups of letters added to the beginnings of words to change their meaning. As you read each word, highlight the prefix and tell what the word means. Then, think of another word that has almost the same meaning and write it below the word." (answers below)

word	prefix	meaning	synonym
disappear	dis-	to fade from view	vanish
unhook	un-	to take off a hook	unfasten

word	prefix	meaning	synonym
rewrite	re-	to write again; to edit	revise
nonsense	non-	without meaning	meaningless

5. Give the student a copy of page 135. Say, "In Column A, you will see words that can be used as the subject of a sentence. In Column B, you will see words that indicate possession. Draw a line from Column A to Column B to match word pairs. Then, use both words in one sentence." (Answers: I/my, we/our, she/hers, he/his)

Grade Level 6

1. Give the student a copy of page 136. Say, "An adverb helps to give detail and exactness to writing. Adverbs are formed by adding -ly to an adjective.

   "Add an adverb to each sentence to tell in what manner the action was performed. Bracket the adjective from which you formed the adverb with your red pen." (Answers: [loud]ly, [slow]ly, [soft]ly)

2. Give the student a copy of page 136. Say, "Jack London wrote a story called the *King of Mazy May*. The word *Mazy* has its source from the word *maze*.

   "Draw a maze on your paper with your red pen. Then, decide how a river could be compared to a maze. Write three main facts pertaining to this idea on the lines below."

3. Give the student a copy of page 137. Say, "A conflict is a struggle between opposing forces. Choose a story you have read and answer these questions about the conflict." (Answers will vary.)

4. Give the student a copy of page 137. Say, "Many words have more than one meaning. For example, if you were to look up the word *saw* in the dictionary, you would see that it has at least two definitions: 'a tool for cutting' and 'an action performed with your eyes.'

   "Look up the meaning of the words on your paper. For each word, write two sentences using a different meaning of the word in each." (Answers will vary.)

5. Give the student a copy of page 138. Say, "Figurative language is used to describe and to make vivid descriptions of people, places, and/or things. After reading the following figurative expressions, name the two things that are being compared. What does each comparison help you to visualize?" (Answers: sail on the dingy vs. wounded seabird's wing; froth of the ocean vs. vine tendrils)

Grade Level 7

1. Give the student a copy of page 138. Say, "In order to draw a good conclusion, we must have enough facts to help with our thinking. Conclusions can also be called *inferences*.

   Read the facts on your paper. On the lines below each fact, write a major inference you can draw from the fact." (Answers: A duck is trapped among the thorn bushes; There is a fire ahead.)

2. Have a book with a glossary available. Give the student a copy of page 139. Say, "Many books contain a glossary at the back to explain the way some words are used in that particular book. Use this book to find the pronunciation and meaning of three of the words. Then, write your own sentence for each word on the lines below." (Answers will vary.)

3. Give the student a copy of page 139. Say, "These sentences describe different stories that might be written about a character named Mr. Amos. From the list that follows the sentences, choose the title that best fits each story. Write the letter of the title on the line next to the sentence." (Answers: 2, 3, 1)

4. Give the student a copy of page 140. Say, "Decide whether these statements contain realistic or fantastic details. For each statement, write *realistic* or *fantastic* on the line on the right." (Answers: a. fantastic, b. fantastic, c. realistic)

5. Give the student a copy of page 140. Say, "Match each word in the left column with its definition in the right column. Write the letter of the definition on the line next to the word it defines." (Answers: c, b, a)

Grade Level 8

1. Give the student a copy of page 141. Say, "A compound sentence is one sentence that has several closely-related ideas in it. By combining important ideas, the writer eliminates several choppy sentences. A compound sentence uses commas to separate each independent clause and a conjunction such as *and, but, for,* or *yet* to link the clauses together.

   "As you read these compound sentences, substitute a period for the commas and the conjunctions. Then, write two compound sentences of your own. Finally, rewrite your two compound sentences, eliminating the commas and conjunctions to create choppy sentences." (Answers on page 125; generated sentences will vary.)

Kenya pretended her feelings weren't hurt. The tears rolled down her cheeks.

I rushed across the room. Then, someone grabbed my arm from behind.

2. Tell the student, "When a word is personified, it is given a human characteristic. Listen to the following sentences as I read them. Decide if the target word has been personified. If it has been, explain how it was personified."

   Present each target word before you read the sentence. Say, "The target word is ____."

   The deep **woods** showed him its dark and secret face. (The woods has a face.)

   Dark cypress **trees** stood quiet, listening as if they were fixated on hearing something important. (The trees have ears to listen.)

   Never kill a **porcupine**. (no personification)

3. Give the student a copy of page 141. Say, "Irony is often used in literature. Read these sentences and explanations. Discuss why irony is part of the format. Then, think of two other sentences or ideas to illustrate irony." (Answers will vary.)

4. Give the student a copy of page 142. Say, "Read a passage aloud from a story of your choice. Then, summarize what you have read. Next, make a prediction about what you think will happen next. Then, silently read a few more paragraphs to see if your prediction was correct." (Answers will vary.)

5. Give the student a copy of page 142. Say, "First, match the words on this page to the definitions that you think will match. Then, use the dictionary to confirm or correct your thinking. Finally, write a sentence to illustrate your knowledge of two of the words." (Answers: 1. c, 2. e, 3. a, 4. b, 5. d)

Understanding Directions

Name _____

Listen to your teacher's directions.

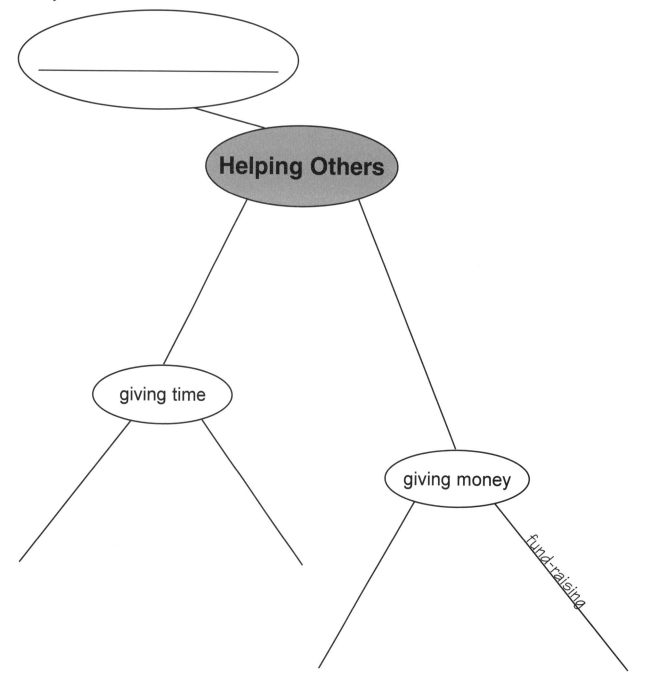

Understanding Directions

Name _____

Listen to your teacher's directions.

1. John got up _____ in the morning.
   early   bright

2. Corn was growing in the _____.
   field   house

3. Grandpa _____ the wagon that was full of wood.
   hit   pulled

4. Are you _____?
   sure   bed

5. I _____ he is telling the truth.
   Molly   believe

Understanding Directions

Name _____

Listen to your teacher's directions.

Box A
scr
spl
str
spr

Box B		
all	awl	eam
ung	ain	are
een	ing	ap
ay	int	

_____   _____   _____

_____   _____   _____

_____   _____   _____

_____   _____   _____

Understanding Directions

Name _____

Listen to your teacher's directions.

_____ Put a plant in each corner.

_____ Put a cricket in the center of the bowl.

_____ Put dirt on top of the gravel.

_____ Feed the cricket with three apple slices.

_____ Get a fish aquarium.

Understanding Directions

Name _____

Listen to your teacher's directions.

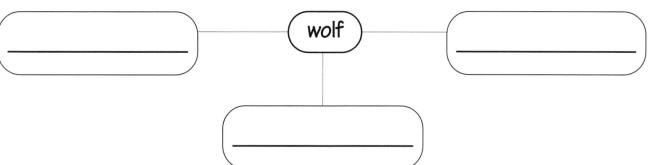

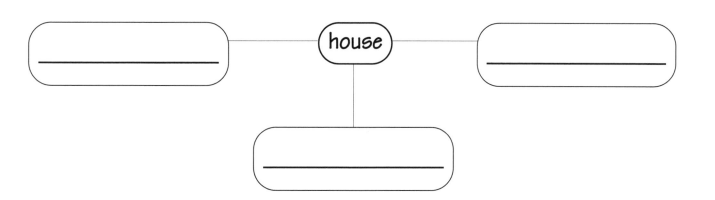

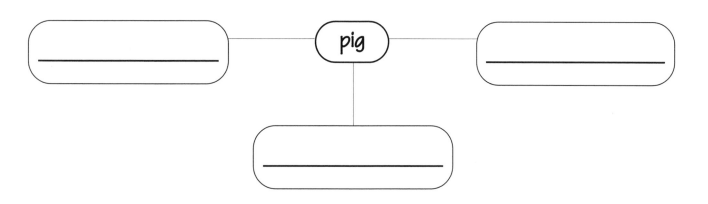

Understanding Directions

Name _____

Listen to your teacher's directions.

```
Word List
lost      cost
frost     Boston
```

1. At the mall, I wandered away from my mom, and soon I was _____.

2. How much does that wagon _____?

3. Our family took a trip to _____.

4. In the winter, we see _____ on the windows.

Understanding Directions

Name _____

Listen to your teacher's directions.

a. The man stepped into the canoe and paddled up to the traffic light at the corner of Main Street and Roberts Road.

b. The dolphin jumped through the hoop at Sea World.

c. The wolves got into the elevator of the large hotel so they could get to their rooms for a nap.

d. It was midnight and the sun was shining so brightly, I had to put on my sunglasses before I went out to play.

e. The boy rode his bike on the side of the road last Saturday morning.

f. We ate dinner at 5:00 and decided to sit on the patio because it was a beautiful evening.

Understanding Directions

Listen to your teacher's directions.

Column A	Column B
airport	screwdriver
waterfront	underline
headline	newsprint
newspaper	airline
screwball	watermelon

Understanding Directions

Listen to your teacher's directions.

echoes	buffalo
echoes echoes echoes echoes echoes	
shelter	necklace
shaggy	longer

Understanding Directions

Name _____

Listen to your teacher's directions.

a. He ___is___ at my house.

b. I ___ride___ in the car.

c. I ___eat___ cookies.

d. They ___are___ going home.

e. I ___write___ my name on the paper.

f. I ___shake___ the dust cloth.

was
wrote
ate
were
rode
shook

Understanding Directions

Name _____

Listen to your teacher's directions.

ā	ail	ain	ay
1. _____	_____	_____	_____
2. _____	_____	_____	_____

Understanding Directions

Name _____

Listen to your teacher's directions.

saw ➡	
glasses ➡	
bark ➡	
rock ➡	
pit ➡	

Understanding Directions

Listen to your teacher's directions.

disappear   rewrite

_____   _____

unhook   nonsense

_____   _____

Understanding Directions

Name _____

Listen to your teacher's directions.

	Column A	**Column B**
	I	his
	we	our
	she	my
	he	hers

Sentences

1. _____

2. _____

3. _____

4. _____

Understanding Directions

Name _____

Listen to your teacher's directions.

When the lion was disturbed, it roared _____.

The man rode _____ to follow the herd of elephants.

The old man mumbled _____.

Understanding Directions

Name _____

Listen to your teacher's directions.

Facts

1. _____

2. _____

3. _____

Understanding Directions

Listen to your teacher's directions.

What gave rise to the conflict?

_____

_____

How is the conflict resolved?

_____

_____

Did the conflict seem realistic? Do you think it would happen in real life? Explain your answer.

_____

_____

Understanding Directions

Name _____

Listen to your teacher's directions.

stake

1. _____

2. _____

rattle

1. _____

2. _____

list

1. _____

2. _____

Understanding Directions

Name _____

Listen to your teacher's directions.

Far from the shore, they spotted a fisherman's dingy, its sail flapping like

the wings of a wounded seabird.

As the pelican disappeared beneath the rough surf, little tendrils of froth

tore at its feathers.

Understanding Directions

Name _____

Listen to your teacher's directions.

Fact:

John stopped pedaling his bike when he heard a sad-sounding quack coming
from the thorn bushes on the side of the road.

Inference:

_____

_____

Fact:

Sue was walking on the path when she suddenly smelled smoke and looked up
to see a darkness in the sky ahead.

Inference:

_____

_____

Understanding Directions

Name _____

Listen to your teacher's directions.

Word _____

Sentence _____

_____

Word _____

Sentence _____

_____

Word _____

Sentence _____

_____

- -

Understanding Directions

Name _____

Listen to your teacher's directions.

_____ Mr. Amos keeps a lizard in a cage. When the lizard escapes, Mr. Amos understands its need for freedom.

_____ Mr. Amos uses his three wishes. In the third wish, he turns the lizard into a cat.

_____ Mr. Amos turns his lizard into a cat but doesn't turn him back into a lizard again, even though he knows it is unhappy as a cat.

Titles

1. The Lizard That Could Purr

2. The Unusual Pet

3. The Three Wishes

Understanding Directions

Name _____

Listen to your teacher's directions.

a. The lizard looked at Mr. Amos with hate in its eyes. _____

b. He offered to turn the cat into a lizard again. _____

c. The neighbors were surprised at Mr. Amos's contentment. _____

Understanding Directions

Name _____

Listen to your teacher's directions.

_____ cunningly   a. wet and dirty

_____ consolation   b. soothing, comforting

_____ bedraggled   c. slyly

Understanding Directions

Listen to your teacher's directions.

Kenya pretended her feelings weren't hurt, yet the tears rolled down her cheeks.

I rushed across the room, and then someone grabbed my arm from behind.

Compound Sentences

_____

_____

Simple Sentences

_____

_____

- -

Understanding Directions

Name _____

Listen to your teacher's directions.

A prisoner is referred to as a "compulsory guest" in a story about prison reform.

Eight hundred dollars is referred to as "a scant $800" in a story that was written in the early 1900's.

Sentences with Irony

_____

_____

_____

_____

Understanding Directions

Name _____

Listen to your teacher's directions.

Summary: _____

_____

_____

_____

Prediction: _____

_____

_____

- -

Understanding Directions

Name _____

Listen to your teacher's directions.

_____ 1. livery buggy   a. a beautiful bird in Egyptian mythology

_____ 2. platform   b. police

_____ 3. phoenix   c. a horse and carriage for hire

_____ 4. rogue catchers   d. partners in crime

_____ 5. confederates   e. statement of intention

Sentence 1 _____

_____

Sentence 2 _____

_____

Developing Note-Taking Skills . . . .

In this section, the student listens to typical classroom lectures and checks the key words in each lecture as she hears them. (Additional words are also listed as foils.) The student then writes a brief summary of the lecture, using the list of key words. Younger students may present their summaries of the lectures orally rather than in writing.

Grade Level 2

1. Vaccines (word list on page 148)

   Because of vaccines, some diseases are no longer a terrible threat to human health. A vaccine is created when weakened or dead, disease-causing organisms are injected into the body. Sometimes a vaccine is specially manufactured from chemical toxins.

   Once the body senses the vaccine, it manufactures antibodies to fight these organisms. The body produces special proteins to make the antibodies. The invading organisms are called "antigens," which means "foreign substance." Our antibodies are like a police force in that they circulate in the bloodstream and attack any antigens that could harm us. Often, we call antigens "bacteria, viruses," or "germs."

2. Solids and Liquids (word list on page 149)

   Solids and liquids are two different states of matter. Matter is in a state we call a "solid" if it has a defined shape and it takes up a definite amount of space. Examples of solids are clothing, furniture, and rocks. The particles that make up a solid are packed together very tightly and have minimal movement. These particles are so tiny that they cannot be seen by our eyes.

   When matter is in a state we call a "liquid," it does not have a defined shape. However, like a solid, it occupies a definite amount of space. Examples of liquids are water, milk, and oil. The tiny particles that make up a liquid are packed together loosely and have great freedom of movement. Because of this freedom of movement, a liquid always takes the shape of its container.

Grade Level 3

1. Protein (word list on page 150)

   Today, we're going to talk about protein. Protein is the second most important element in the body (water is first). We get complete proteins from fish, eggs, milk, and meat. We get combined, incomplete proteins from foods such as black beans and rice, rice and lentils, or tuna salad with pita bread. Once protein molecules are inside the body, they are broken down into amino acids, which are commonly called "the building blocks of the body." We need these amino acids to repair tissues and to support growth. Enzymes in the digestive system help the proteins to form amino acids.

2. Environment (word list on page 151)

When we think of the environment, we think of everything that surrounds us and affects us. All living things survive best in the environment that is best suited for them. If a living creature is placed in an environment that is unsuitable for its species, it might die. For example, all fish require a water environment. However, some fish, such as dolphins and sharks, require a saltwater environment. Other fish, such as trout and stripers, require a fresh-water environment. Some water animals, such as shrimp and moray eels, live at the bottom of their water environment. Other water animals, such as dolphins and flying fish, like to be closer to the surface of the water.

Grade Level 4

1. African Savanna (word list on page 152)

A savanna is a grassland found in tropical climates such as Africa, India, and Australia. The grassland has very few trees and bushes and is a wide-open area populated by many interacting animals. Some of the animals feed directly on the grasses. Zebras eat the tops of the grasses, gazelles nibble on the bottom parts of the grasses, and wildebeests eat the middle sections of the grasses. Other animals feed on the grass-eaters. Crocodiles attack and eat wildebeests as they attempt to cross rivers. Lions hunt zebras and gazelles.

2. Wind Erosion (word list on page 153)

Wind has the ability to reshape our land. Strong winds carry sediments, such as sand and soil, from one area to another. This process is called "wind erosion." During periods of drought, when vegetation dies, more soil is exposed to the potential damages of wind. At this time windbreakers, such as fences, can slow down the effects of the wind. As the wind moves sediment along the ground, the grains of sand and dirt in the sediment act as sandblasters, chipping, cutting, and polishing surfaces on the earth. These sediments are dropped when the wind hits a large object such as a large rock or a bush. If enough sediment falls in the same area, a dune can form. A dune, simply, is a pile or hill of sand. We commonly see dunes when we go to the beach or look at pictures of a desert.

Grade Level 5

1. Herbivore, Carnivore, or Omnivore? (word list on page 154)

The Brontosaurus Rex is a well-known example of a herbivore, a plant-eating animal. The Tyrannosaurus Rex is a well-known example of a carnivore, a meat-eating animal. People are definitely omnivores because we eat plants and meat. Other examples of herbivores include squirrels, deer, gazelles, cows, and manatees. In fact, manatees are often called "the cows of the underwater world." The family of carnivores includes owls, wolves, cats, and alligators. These animals feed on the food chain. Owls, for example, eat the smaller mice, while wolves love to munch on a mouthful of owl. Omnivores include turtles and birds, including chickens. If you spent a day with a bird, you would find it nibbling on worms in the morning, feasting on seeds and berries throughout the day, and finally settling for a bedtime snack of bugs.

2. Photosynthesis (word list on page 155)

The word *photosynthesis* pertains to a plant's ability to use light to make its own food. Specifically, energy from light allows the plant to combine carbon dioxide, a gas from the air, and water. This process produces glucose, a form of sugar used by plants for food. Carbon dioxide enters the plant through tiny holes on the underside of the plant's leaves. Water enters the plant via the roots. Chlorophyll, the green pigment in the plants, collects light energy from the sun.

A very important byproduct of photosynthesis is the production of oxygen. Every living organism on Earth requires oxygen in order to survive. The oxygen made by plants leaves through the same little holes that let the carbon dioxide into the plant.

Grade Level 6

1. Metric System (word list on page 156)

The *metric system* is called the "scientific system of measurement" because it is used by scientists all over the world. The metric system is a decimal system just like our number system and is used to measure everything.

When measuring the length of an object, scientists speak of "meters." For example, a piece of lumber might be two meters long. When measuring the volume of something, scientists speak of "liters." For example, you might buy a two-liter bottle of soda. When measuring temperature, scientists speak of "Celsius." For example, water boils at 100° Celsius.

2. Microscopes (word list on page 157)

Microscopes use light rays and curved pieces of glass called "lenses" to produce enlarged images of an object. A magnifying glass is a very simple microscope that uses only one lens.

A microscope that is used in science classes is called a "compound light microscope." This instrument has two lenses and can magnify an object up to 1,000 times its actual size. When a microscope uses the beams of tiny particles called "electrons," it is called an "electron microscope." This type of microscope is so powerful that it can magnify an object up to one million times its actual size.

Grade Level 7

1. The Ocean Floor (word list on page 158)

    One of the major features of the ocean floor is called the "Abyssal Plains." The plains are large, flat areas covered by sediment that rivers have deposited into oceans. The plains of the Atlantic and Indian Oceans are larger than the plains of the Pacific Ocean. The world's greatest rivers flow into these two oceans. The Mississippi, Congo, Nile, and Amazon Rivers flow into the Atlantic Ocean, and the Ganges and Indus Rivers flow into the Indian Ocean.

    Another feature of the ocean floor is seamounts, which are underwater mountains. In order for a mountain to be a seamount, it must be at least 1,000 meters tall, have steep sides, and have a narrow top called a "summit." When a seamount reaches above the water, it is called an "island." The island of Hawaii, a well-known seamount, is the highest seamount on Earth. It is more that 9,600 meters high.

2. Groundwater (word list on page 159)

    Water stored in the ground is called "groundwater" and is accessible only when pumped out of the ground. This water gathers as a result of precipitation— rain, snow, hail, or sleet. The water hits the ground and moves down slowly through the dirt and rocks until it reaches an area that will allow no further downward movement. This area is usually dense rock or clay and is referred to as an "impermeable area"—an area that doesn't allow any water movement. This impermeable area acts like a basin, and the water fills within it. Areas that allow for water movement are called "permeable areas." Examples of permeable material include dirt, gravel, and sandstone.

Grade Level 8

1. Sponges (word list on page 160)

    Sponges are often regarded as plants because they have minimal movement. They attach themselves to a spot and stay there for life, unless they are displaced by a strong wave or current. Actually, sponges are the most ancient animals in existence today. They are a simple form of life in the invertebrate family and usually reside in salt water. A very few species of sponge live in the freshwater environment of streams and lakes.

    Sponges are classified as Porifera (poh-RIHF-er-uh) because their bodies are covered with tiny openings called "pores." Water enters into these pores, bringing the sponge food and oxygen. The sponge cells remove the nutrients and release waste products in the form of carbon dioxide and undigested food. These waste products leave the sponge through larger pores.

2. Reptiles (word list on page 161)

Turtles, crocodiles, and snakes are several examples of reptiles. Reptiles have several distinct characteristics, the first being skin that is covered by tough, dry scales. These scales are made of material very similar to the human finger-nail. The scales form a waterproof covering that makes it almost impossible for the reptile to lose water. However, this very same waterproofing also makes it impossible for the reptile to breathe through its skin. Therefore, the reptile is totally dependent upon its lungs for breathing.

Another characteristic of the reptile is its special eggs. The egg is surrounded by a flexible, yet tough, shell that somewhat resembles a piece of leather. This shell prevents the inner contents from drying out. The shell looks solid but is actually a mass of tiny pores. These pores allow gases to move in and out but prevent water loss.

Prosody Training . . . .

Students presenting with deficits in central auditory processing may reflect difficulties with the pragmatic aspects of communication. They may misunderstand the nuances of language that are conveyed via subtle changes in intonation, stress, and rhythm patterns. The exercises in this section focus on helping the student strengthen skills for under-standing how changes in syllabic stress can affect the meaning of words.

Level 1: Syllabic Stress in Words

Copy pages 162 and 163 to introduce these words and definitions to your student to make sure the student knows what each word looks like, sounds like, and means. Be sure the student understands that the meaning of each word changes as the syllabic stress is changed. The boldfaced type indicates the stressed syllable in each word. Present a word and its definition. Then, have the student imitate your model by pronouncing the word and giving its definition.

Level 2: Syllabic Stress, Mixed Order

In this task, the words from Level 1 (pages 162-163) are presented individ-ually in mixed order. Again, the student repeats the word that you said and then defines it. Some possible modifications include the following:

a. For younger students or students with weak vocabulary skills, feel free to omit the requirement to define each word.

b. Provide the student with the handout from Level 1 (pages 162-163) so she can scan the list to find definitions as necessary.

c. Work with word meanings may be omitted completely. *(continued on page 164)*

Taking Notes

Name _____

Check each key word from the lecture. Then, use the words you have checked to write a summary of the lecture.

Vaccines

___ vaccines	___ organisms	___ to	___ circulate
___ diseases	___ are	___ fight	___ bloodstream
___ threat	___ injected	___ proteins	___ attack
___ human	___ the	___ make	___ could
___ health	___ body	___ invading	___ harm
___ is	___ manufactured	___ antigens	___ us
___ created	___ toxins	___ foreign substance	___ bacteria
___ weakened	___ senses	___ like	___ viruses
___ dead	___ antibodies	___ police force	___ germs

_____

_____

_____

_____

_____

_____

_____

_____

_____

_____

Taking Notes

Name _____

Check each key word from the lecture. Then, use the words you have checked to write a summary of the lecture.

Solids and Liquids

___ different	___ amount	___ minimal	___ milk
___ states	___ space	___ movement	___ oil
___ matter	___ clothing	___ tiny	___ loosely
___ solid	___ furniture	___ they	___ freedom
___ it	___ rocks	___ seen	___ always
___ has	___ particles	___ eyes	___ shape
___ defined	___ packed	___ liquid	___ for
___ shape	___ tightly	___ not	___ container
___ definite	___ and	___ water	___ rocks

_____

_____

_____

_____

_____

_____

_____

_____

_____

_____

Taking Notes

Check each key word from the lecture. Then, use the words you have checked to write a summary of the lecture.

Protein

___ protein	___ complete	___ with	___ support
___ second	___ fish	___ molecules	___ growth
___ important	___ eggs	___ broken	___ enzymes
___ element	___ combined	___ amino acids	___ digestive system
___ body	___ from	___ building blocks	___ be
___ and	___ black beans	___ repair	___ form
___ water	___ rice	___ tissues	
___ first	___ or	___ if	

_____

_____

_____

_____

_____

_____

_____

_____

_____

_____

_____

_____

Taking Notes

Name _____

Check each key word from the lecture. Then, use the words you have checked to write a summary of the lecture.

Environment

___ environment	___ suited	___ die	___ moray eels
___ everything	___ for	___ fish	___ bottom
___ surrounds	___ creature	___ water	___ their
___ affects	___ placed	___ saltwater	___ dolphins
___ all	___ that	___ trout	___ surface
___ living	___ unsuitable	___ freshwater	
___ survive	___ species	___ shrimp	

_____

_____

_____

_____

_____

_____

_____

_____

_____

_____

_____

Taking Notes

Name _____

Check each key word from the lecture. Then, use the words you have checked to write a summary of the lecture.

African Savanna

___ African   ___ bushes   ___ gazelles   ___ attack

___ grassland ___ wide-open ___ nibble   ___ cross

___ in   ___ by   ___ bottom   ___ rivers

___ tropical   ___ animals   ___ wildebeests ___ lions

___ climates   ___ feed   ___ the   ___ hunt

___ Africa   ___ grasses   ___ middle

___ few   ___ zebras   ___ grass-eaters

___ trees   ___ tops   ___ crocodiles

_____

_____

_____

_____

_____

_____

_____

_____

_____

_____

_____

_____

Taking Notes

Name _____

Check each key word from the lecture. Then, use the words you have checked to write a summary of the lecture.

Wind Erosion

___ wind	___ another	___ windbreakers	___ dropped
___ ability	___ erosion	___ fences	___ large
___ reshape	___ drought	___ slow	___ falls
___ land	___ vegetation	___ moves	___ dune
___ strong	___ dies	___ along	___ commonly
___ carry	___ soil	___ ground	___ beach
___ sediments	___ exposed	___ grains	___ look
___ sand	___ of	___ sandblasters	___ pictures
___ one area	___ at	___ polishing	___ desert

_____

_____

_____

_____

_____

_____

_____

_____

_____

_____

_____

Taking Notes

Name _____

Check each key word from the lecture. Then, use the words you have checked to write a summary of the lecture.

Herbivore, Carnivore, or Omnivore?

___ Brontosaurus	___ meat-eating	___ owls	___ chickens
___ herbivore	___ people	___ wolves	___ bedtime
___ plant-eating	___ omnivores	___ cats	___ bugs
___ Tyrannosaurus	___ deer	___ alligators	
___ another	___ cows	___ food chain	
___ carnivore	___ manatees	___ smaller	

_____

_____

_____

_____

_____

_____

_____

_____

_____

_____

_____

_____

Taking Notes

Name _____

Check each key word from the lecture. Then, use the words you have checked to write a summary of the lecture.

Photosynthesis

___ photosynthesis	___ water	___ underside	___ byproduct
___ plant's ability	___ process	___ leaves	___ production
___ specifically	___ glucose	___ via	___ oxygen
___ energy	___ form	___ roots	___ found
___ light	___ sugar	___ chlorophyll	___ survive
___ combine	___ food	___ green	___ same
___ carbon dioxide	___ enters	___ pigment	___ that
___ gas	___ tiny	___ collects	
___ air	___ holes	___ sun	

_____

_____

_____

_____

_____

_____

_____

_____

_____

_____

_____

Taking Notes

Name _____

Check each key word from the lecture. Then, use the words you have checked to write a summary of the lecture.

Metric System

___ metric system	___ decimal	___ meters	___ temperature
___ called	___ many	___ piece	___ Celsius
___ scientific	___ everything	___ lumber	___ example
___ measurement	___ length	___ volume	___ water
___ because	___ object	___ liters	___ boils
___ world	___ speak	___ soda	___ system

_____

_____

_____

_____

_____

_____

_____

_____

_____

_____

_____

Taking Notes

Check each key word from the lecture. Then, use the words you have checked to write a summary of the lecture.

Microscopes

___ microscopes	___ enlarged	___ compound light	___ beams
___ light rays	___ images	___ two lenses	___ particles
___ curved	___ an	___ 1,000 times	___ electrons
___ pieces	___ magnifying	___ actual	___ powerful
___ glass	___ simple	___ size	___ object
___ lenses	___ one lens	___ when	___ one million times

_____

_____

_____

_____

_____

_____

_____

_____

_____

_____

_____

Taking Notes

Name _____

Check each key word from the lecture. Then, use the words you have checked to write a summary of the lecture.

The Ocean Floor

___ major	___ deposited	___ seamounts	___ water
___ features	___ Atlantic	___ underwater	___ called
___ Abyssal Plains	___ more	___ mountains	___ island
___ large	___ Pacific Ocean	___ 1,000 meters	___ Hawaii
___ flat	___ greatest	___ steep	___ highest
___ covered	___ Mississippi	___ summit	___ 9,600 meters
___ sediment	___ Nile	___ reaches	
___ rivers	___ Ganges	___ above	

_____

_____

_____

_____

_____

_____

_____

_____

_____

_____

_____

Taking Notes

Name _____

Check each key word from the lecture. Then, use the words you have checked to write a summary of the lecture.

Groundwater

___ stored	___ hits	___ dense	___ movement
___ accessible	___ slowly	___ clay	___ permeable
___ only	___ through	___ impermeable	___ examples
___ pumped	___ dirt	___ area	___ material
___ gathers	___ rocks	___ doesn't	___ gravel
___ precipitation	___ area	___ like	___ sandstone
___ rain	___ no	___ basin	
___ snow	___ downward	___ fills	

_____

_____

_____

_____

_____

_____

_____

_____

_____

_____

Taking Notes

Name _____

Check each key word from the lecture. Then, use the words you have checked to write a summary of the lecture.

Sponges

___ plants	___ ancient	___ few	___ bringing
___ minimal	___ animals	___ species	___ food
___ movement	___ existence	___ freshwater	___ oxygen
___ attach	___ simple	___ classified	___ waste
___ stay	___ form	___ Porifera	___ carbon dioxide
___ life	___ invertebrate	___ bodies	___ undigested food
___ displaced	___ usually	___ openings	___ leave
___ current	___ reside	___ water	___ larger
___ actually	___ salt water	___ enters	___ pores

_____

_____

_____

_____

_____

_____

_____

_____

_____

_____

_____

Taking Notes

Name _____

Check each key word from the lecture. Then, use the words you have checked to write a summary of the lecture.

Reptiles

___ turtles   ___ waterproof   ___ eggs   ___ mass

___ characteristics   ___ impossible   ___ flexible   ___ pores

___ skin   ___ lose   ___ leather   ___ gases

___ tough   ___ water   ___ inner   ___ move

___ dry   ___ breathe   ___ contents   ___ prevent

___ scales   ___ dependent   ___ drying   ___ loss

___ human   ___ lungs   ___ looks

___ fingernail   ___ special   ___ solid

_____

_____

_____

_____

_____

_____

_____

_____

_____

_____

Syllabic Stress in Words

Name _____

The words in these pairs are spelled alike, but they are pronounced differently. The stressed syllable is boldfaced.

1. **af**fect — feeling
   af**fect** — to influence

2. com**bine** — to join things together
   combine — a harvesting machine

3. **com**mune — a group of people living together
   com**mune** — to exchange thoughts and feelings

4. **com**pact — an agreement
   com**pact** — closely packed

5. com**pound** — to combine
   compound — an enclosed yard

6. com**press** — to squeeze together
   compress — a soft, folded gauze or cloth pad

7. con**duct** — to direct or lead
   conduct — behavior

8. con**serve** — to protect from loss; to avoid wasting
   conserve — jam

9. **con**sole — a cabinet
   con**sole** — to soothe or comfort

10. **con**tent — all things inside
    con**tent** — satisfied

11. **con**test — competition
    con**test** — to try to disprove

12. **con**tract — an agreement
    con**tract** — to shrink

13. con**verse** — to talk
    converse — opposite

14. **de**fect — a flaw
    de**fect** — to forsake or become a traitor

Name _____

The words in these pairs are spelled alike, but they are pronounced differently. The stressed syllable is boldfaced.

15. **de**sert   a hot, dry, sandy place
    de**sert**   to abandon

16. **en**trance   a place to go inside
    en**trance**   to delight or charm

17. es**say**   to try
    essay   a short piece of writing

18. **in**cense   perfume for burning
    in**cense**   to infuriate

19. **in**tern   a medical student
    in**tern**   to confine

20. in**val**id   wrong
    invalid   someone who is sickly or disabled

21. **ob**ject   a thing
    ob**ject**   to complain

22. of**fense**   an insult
    offense   the aggressive team in an athletic game

23. **pre**sent   a gift
    pre**sent**   to introduce

24. pro**ceed**   to go forward
    proceed   income

25. **pro**duce   fruits and vegetables
    pro**duce**   to yield

26. **pro**ject   a planned undertaking
    pro**ject**   to throw forward

27. re**coil**   to fall back under pressure
    recoil   a reaction; a kickback

28. re**fuse**   to say no
    refuse   garbage

163

Level 2: Syllabic Stress, Mixed Order *(continued from page 147)*

1. **af**fect — feeling
2. **com**mune — a group of people living together
3. con**duct** — to direct or lead
4. **con**test — competition
5. **en**trance — a place to go inside
6. in**val**id — wrong
7. **re**coil — a reaction; a kickback
8. es**say** — to try
9. **con**sole — a cabinet
10. **de**fect — a flaw
11. com**bine** — to join things together
12. in**cense** — to infuriate
13. **pre**sent — a gift
14. con**serve** — to protect from loss; to avoid wasting
15. **pro**ject — a planned undertaking
16. **con**tract — an agreement
17. pro**ceed** — to go forward
18. re**fuse** — to say no
19. **pro**duce — fruits and vegetables
20. **con**tent — all things inside
21. **com**pound — an enclosed yard
22. **com**pact — an agreement
23. **in**tern — a medical student
24. **con**duct — behavior
25. **de**sert — a hot, dry, sandy place
26. en**trance** — to delight or charm
27. com**press** — to squeeze together
28. con**test** — to try to disprove
29. de**fect** — to forsake or become a traitor
30. con**sole** — to soothe or comfort
31. **in**valid — someone who is sickly or disabled
32. con**verse** — to talk
33. **es**say — a short piece of writing
34. **af**fect — to influence
35. re**coil** — to fall back under pressure
36. **ob**ject — a thing
37. pre**sent** — to introduce

38. **ref**use	garbage
39. **pro**ceed	income
40. **of**fense	an insult
41. com**pact**	closely packed
42. pro**ject**	to throw forward
43. ob**ject**	to complain
44. **com**press	a soft, folded gauze or cloth pad
45. con**tract**	to shrink
46. **com**bine	a harvesting machine
47. **con**serve	jam
48. **con**verse	opposite
49. com**pound**	to combine
50. in**tern**	to confine
51. de**sert**	to abandon
52. con**tent**	satisfied
53. **in**cense	perfume for burning
54. **of**fense	the aggressive team in an athletic game
55. com**mune**	to exchange thoughts and feelings
56. pro**duce**	to yield

Level 3: Words in Sentences

Read each sentence to the student. Ask the student to determine which word is used in the sentence by listening for both syllabic stress and contextual clues. Provide the handout on pages 162-163 only for those who need the information as a guide.

1. The girl's affect led me to believe one thing, but when she spoke, I immediately changed my impression. (**af**fect)

2. Ann had the choice of living in an apartment by herself or living in the commune with her friends. (**com**mune)

3. He spent many years in school learning how to conduct an orchestra. (con**duct**)

4. Tina entered the contest with hopes of winning first prize. (**con**test)

5. They walked into the entrance of the building. (**en**trance)

6. His entry for the science fair was invalid because it was submitted a week past the cut-off date. (in**val**id)

7. The president's vacation home is a compound in Maine. (**com**pound)

8. We watched them essay crossing the rapids. (es**say**)

9. They stored the extra books and stereo equipment in the console. (**con**sole)

10. Since the table had a defect, I returned it to the store. (**de**fect)

11. I will combine all the ingredients to make the cake. (com**bine**)

12. She felt incensed when she received an *F* on her exam. (in**censed**)

13. I got four presents for my birthday. (**pre**sents)

14. On the island of Bermuda, it is very important to conserve fresh water. (con**serve**)

15. He finished his project two weeks earlier than planned. (**pro**ject)

16. We drew up the contract for the sale yesterday. (**con**tract)

17. The traffic officer waved his hand, indicating that the cars could proceed across the bridge. (pro**ceed**)

18. I wanted to refuse another piece of cake because I was feeling quite plump. (re**fuse**)

19. Every time I enter the grocery store, I go to the produce section first. (**pro**duce)

20. The police officer opened my letter and examined the content. (**con**tent)

21. Her mother objected to the way she colored her hair. (ob**ject**ed)

22. The two men finished their compact with a handshake. (**com**pact)

23. The intern arrived at the accident before the ambulance. (**in**tern)

24. Because the child's conduct was so unmanageable, he had to stay after school. (**con**duct)

25. We saw four camels in the desert. (**de**sert)

26. We were entranced by the puppet show. (en**tranced**)

27. I put the aluminum pan into the machine so it could be compressed before I threw it into the recycling bin. (com**pressed**)

28. The lawyer was a specialist when it came to contesting settlements. (con**test**ing)

29. The spy wanted to defect from his country. (de**fect**)

30. The springs in this mattress have strong recoil. (**re**coil)

31. We built a ramp for the invalid so he could enter the house without leaving his wheelchair. (**in**valid)

32. The young Italian students tried to converse in English, but it was too difficult for them. (con**verse**)

33. Ian wrote an essay about the ozone layer. (**es**say)

34. How will the heavy rain affect the young crops? (a**ffect**)

35. Lisa put a hot compress on her head to try to stop her headache. (**com**press)

36. I found five objects in the box. (**ob**jects)

37. May I present Princess Sarah to you? (pre**sent**)

38. Mike gathered the refuse and put it in the trash. (**ref**use)

39. We counted the proceeds from our bake sale. (**pro**ceeds)

40. Nate took offense when the teacher accused him of cheating. (o**ffense**)

41. I stamped on the dirt to compact it around the tree's roots. (com**pact**)

42. Art used a microphone so his voice would project across the field. (pro**ject**)

43. Every time the soldiers tried to advance, their enemies forced them to recoil. (re**coil**)

44. Some plants have leaves that contract when you touch them. (con**tract**)

45. The farmer rode in the combine for four hours to finish harvesting the wheat. (**com**bine)

46. I love strawberry conserve on biscuits. (**con**serve)

47. My point of view is converse to yours. (**con**verse)

48. The money in my savings account compounds daily. (com**pounds**)

49. The sheriff will intern the accused woman until the judge returns. (in**tern**)

50. "Please don't desert me!" the boy cried to his friend. (de**sert**)

51. The kittens were content after their mother fed them. (con**tent**)

52. Shall we burn incense to repel the mosquitoes? (**in**cense)

53. A good football team needs to play both offense and defense well. (**off**ense)

54. The poet felt the urge to commune with nature. (com**mune**)

55. I will attempt to produce a new product. (pro**duce**)

56. The mother tried to console her baby. (con**sole**)

Level 4: Sentence Pairs

Give the student a copy of the appropriate page (select from pages 169-177) to read as you do this exercise together. Read one sentence from each pair to the student and have her identify which sentence you read. Ask the student to explain how she could tell which of the two sentences you read.

Sentence Pairs

Name _____

Your teacher will read one sentence from each pair. Tell which sentence was read and explain how you knew the answer.

1. a. You mean I scream.
    b. You mean ice cream.

2. a. It's hard to recognize speech.
    b. It's hard to wreck a nice beach.

3. a. The boy buys ink.
    b. The boys buy zinc.

4. a. I heard the night rain.
    b. I heard the night train.

5. a. He took a name.
    b. He took an aim.

6. a. We have a nice chest.
    b. We have an ice chest.

7. a. It's a grade A.
    b. It's a gray day.

8. a. I thought of a notion.
    b. I thought of an ocean.

9. a. I saw a beast of burden.
    b. I saw a pizza burnin'.

10. a. He is a bee feeder.
    b. He is a beef eater.

11. a. They sat on a tack.
    b. They had an attack.

12. a. The night rate was reasonable.
    b. The nitrate was reasonable.

Sentence Pairs

Your teacher will read one sentence from each pair. Tell which sentence was read and explain how you knew the answer.

1. a. The boys are hoarse.
    b. The boy's a horse.

2. a. She heard a music album.
    b. She heard a musical bum.

3. a. This guy is falling.
    b. The sky is falling.

4. a. Daniel, close the door.
    b. Dan will close the door.

5. a. The cattle eat it.
    b. The cat'll eat it.

6. a. I don't think their sight or smell's that good.
    b. I don't think their cider smells that good.

7. a. We'll get a mass of cold.
    b. We'll get a massive cold.

8. a. His story was never clear to me.
    b. History was never clear to me.

9. a. I'll have more ice.
    b. I'll have more rice.

10. a. He went to Caesar.
    b. He went to seize her.

11. a. The stuff he knows is annoying.
    b. The stuffy nose is annoying.

12. a. The boy just uttered something.
    b. The boy just stuttered something.

Sentence Pairs

Your teacher will read one sentence from each pair. Tell which sentence was read and explain how you knew the answer.

1. a. He made a plan for a cedar fence.
   b. He made a plan for a sea defense.

2. a. The children freed Annie.
   b. The children free Danny.

3. a. I saw the giant's eyes there.
   b. I saw the giant size there.

4. a. Give me the great ape.
   b. Give me the gray tape.

5. a. I studied history.
   b. I studied his story.

6. a. She is a homemaker.
   b. She is a hoe maker.

7. a. They shouted, "It sprays!"
   b. They shouted its praise.

8. a. See, it swings.
   b. See its wings.

9. a. "Keep sticking," he said.
   b. "Keeps ticking," he said.

10. a. We may cough later in the day.
    b. We make off later in the day.

11. a. My keys are in the car.
    b. Mikey's are in the car.

12. a. They walked through the pea stalks.
    b. They walked through the peace talks.

Sentence Pairs

Name _____

Your teacher will read one sentence from each pair. Tell which sentence was read and explain how you knew the answer.

1. a. I have a plum pie.
    b. I have a plump eye.

2. a. I see Mable.
    b. I seem able.

3. a. I like to see them eat.
    b. I like to see the meat.

4. a. The vet examined sixty-six sheep.
    b. The vet examined sixty sick sheep.

5. a. He developed a standards-based test.
    b. He developed a standard-spaced test.

6. a. "That's tough," he thought.
    b. "That stuff," he thought.

7. a. She has tulips.
    b. She has two lips.

8. a. Twenty sick swans were in the water.
    b. Twenty-six ones were in the water.

9. a. We'll own a boat.
    b. We loan a boat.

10. a. We have no notions that are imaginable.
    b. We have known oceans that are imaginable.

11. a. We'll leave an' say goodbye to her.
    b. We'll even say goodbye to her.

12. a. Michael, row your boat.
    b. Mike will row your boat.

Sentence Pairs

Name _____

Your teacher will read one sentence from each pair. Tell which sentence was read and explain how you knew the answer.

1. a. I've seen some mothers over there.
    b. I've seen some others over there.

2. a. I jumped the biggest hurdle.
    b. I jumped the biggest turtle.

3. a. White shoes—how golfers love them!
    b. Why choose how golfers love them?

4. a. What is that in the road ahead?
    b. What is that in the road, a head?

5. a. She was a lighthouse keeper.
    b. She was a light housekeeper.

6. a. He was outstanding in the field.
    b. He was out standing in the field.

7. a. They're both a jar.
    b. They're both ajar.

8. a. She's a great grandmother.
    b. She's a great-grandmother.

9. a. After noon is the best time for a nap.
    b. Afternoon is the best time for a nap.

10. a. Go over; throw the ball.
    b. Go overthrow the ball.

11. a. In the cartoon, I saw the rattlesnake around the room.
    b. In the cartoon, I saw the rattle snake around the room.

12. a. Can you see anybody there?
    b. Can you see any body there?

Sentence Pairs

Name _____

Your teacher will read one sentence from each pair. Tell which sentence was read and explain how you knew the answer.

1. a. Is anyone out of place?
   b. Is any one out of place?

2. a. In my dream, I saw the butterfly.
   b. In my dream, I saw the butter fly.

3. a. Anyway, I'll get home.
   b. Any way I'll get home.

4. a. Run to the base, man!
   b. Run to the baseman.

5. a. Four businesswomen work.
   b. For business, women work.

6. a. At the pond, I saw the catfish.
   b. At the pond, I saw the cat fish.

7. a. Look at the cowboy.
   b. Look at the cow, boy.

8. a. Put it near the doorway, down near the bottom.
   b. Put it near the door, way down near the bottom.

9. a. Sweep the driveway before dinner.
   b. Sweep the drive, way before dinner.

10. a. I felt the earth quake.
    b. I felt the earthquake.

11. a. I broke the eggshell and all.
    b. I broke the egg, shell and all.

12. a. Yesterday I saw the fireman.
    b. Yesterday I saw the fire, man.

Sentence Pairs

Your teacher will read one sentence from each pair. Tell which sentence was read and explain how you knew the answer.

1. a. I saw his foot step to the left.
    b. I saw his footstep to the left.

2. a. Because he was a freshman, I avoided him.
    b. Because he was a fresh man, I avoided him.

3. a. He is a grand father.
    b. He is a grandfather.

4. a. I saw the grassland in the distance.
    b. I saw the grass land in the distance.

5. a. I use my handwriting with markers.
    b. I use my hand writing with markers.

6. a. The chief looked at his headdress and moccasins.
    b. The chief looked at his head, dress, and moccasins.

7. a. The pie is homemade by Mom.
    b. The pie is home, made by Mom.

8. a. Catch up with the horse, men.
    b. Catch up with the horsemen.

9. a. She owns a houseboat and car.
    b. She owns a house, boat, and car.

10. a. However, will I get there?
    b. How ever will I get there?

11. a. He painted the lighthouse.
    b. He painted the light house.

12. a. We watched the nightfall around us.
    b. We watched the night fall around us.

Sentence Pairs

Your teacher will read one sentence from each pair. Tell which sentence was read and explain how you knew the answer.

1. a. They used the paintbrush and easel.
    b. They used the paint, brush, and easel.

2. a. I put butter on the pancake and spoon.
    b. I put butter on the pan, cake, and spoon.

3. a. Call the policemen.
    b. Call the police, men.

4. a. I had popcorn and a burger.
    b. I had pop, corn, and a burger.

5. a. Please proofread and type my story.
    b. Please proof, read, and type my story.

6. a. Get the quarterback here.
    b. Get the quarter back here.

7. a. I felt the rain drop on my head.
    b. I felt the raindrop on my head.

8. a. I heard the rain fall on the tin roof.
    b. I heard the rainfall on the tin roof.

9. a. We bought a sail, boat, and anchor.
    b. We bought a sailboat and anchor.

10 a. We had the greatest salesman.
    b. We had the greatest sales, man.

11. a. I picked up some sandstone and gravel.
    b. I picked up some sand, stone, and gravel.

12. a. We study at the school, house, or park.
    b. We study at the schoolhouse or park.

Sentence Pairs

Name _____

Your teacher will read one sentence from each pair. Tell which sentence was read and explain how you knew the answer.

1. a. We visited the seaport and ship.
   b. We visited the sea, port, and ship.

2. a. We saw the seashells and pelicans.
   b. We saw the sea, shells, and pelicans.

3. a. He took pictures of the seashore and cabins.
   b. He took pictures of the sea, shore, and cabins.

4. a. We played with the snowman.
   b. We played with the snow, man.

5. a. He saw the steamboat and paddles.
   b. He saw the steam, boat, and paddles.

6. a. I brought a suitcase full of socks and shoes.
   b. I brought a suit, case full of socks, and shoes.

7. a. See the sunshine.
   b. See the sun shine.

8. a. Fitness is not for everybody.
   b. Fitness is not for every body.

9. a. He stood upright next to me.
   b. He stood up, right next to me.

10. a. We saw the waterfall from the mountain.
    b. We saw the water fall from the mountain.

11. a. I saw the waterway in the distance.
    b. I saw the water way in the distance.

12. a. On the African Safari, I saw wildlife.
    b. On the African Safari, I saw wild life.

Auditory binaural integration involves the ability to integrate information received from a variety of modalities simultaneously. A deficit in this area may affect students' abilities to function within a "whole language" environment, to function within the "centers" of a classroom, or to participate in note-taking activities. Stimulating interhemispheric transfers is one way to help students with a deficit in this area.

Interhemispheric exercises involve verbal-to-motor and motor-to-verbal activities accompanied by lots of repetition. Examples of these activities include singing, feeling objects that are not visible (grab-bag format) and then talking about them, and participating in pencil-and-paper activities where the student "listens and does" and then talks. Students that present with a deficit in this area often respond well to music lessons. Therefore, an activity using a xylophone has been provided for your convenience.

Singing · · · · · · · · · · · · · · · · · · ·

Singing, rhyming, and musical activities are excellent ways to stimulate interhemispheric transfers. Whenever possible, have accompanying music available for the students' use during these activities. Students will engage in a progression of singing activities, beginning with familiar songs.

Level 1: Familiar Songs

Any songs that are familiar to the child and his or her environment are appropriate to use in this section. Whenever possible, have accompanying music available, such as someone playing the piano while everyone sings or playing a tape cassette of the song. This exercise can be introduced during a therapy session and should be continued as a home activity.

Chanting while jumping rope or bouncing a ball is also an excellent activity at this level. An example of chanting is "A, my name is Alice and my husband's name is Al and we live in Alabama and we eat apples. B, ..." Fingerplays work well, too, such as "Where Is Thumbkin?," "Five Little Pumpkins," and "Here Is the Beehive." Here is a list of other common songs:

"Happy Birthday to You"	"This Old Man"
"Row, Row, Row, Your Boat"	"Bingo"
"Mary Had a Little Lamb"	"If You're Happy and You Know It"
"Jingle Bells"	"Deck the Halls"
"Kookaburra"	"Shoo, Fly, Don't Bother Me"
"Skip to My Lou"	"Take Me Out to the Ball Game"

Level 2: Rhyming with Songs

Once the student sings or chants comfortably with materials as suggested in Level 1, introduce rhyming song exercises. In this activity, you and the student can create rhyming songs about activities for daily living, using as many rhyming words as you can. Whenever possible, incorporate gestures to enhance the repetitious nature of the material. Use familiar tunes or make up original songs. You, the student, and family members can have lots of fun with these rhyming activities.

Morning Routine

flush - brush

press - dress

who - shoe

zip - trip

comb - alone

eight - late

sleep - peep

Breakfast

bowl - roll

waffle - awful

egg - beg

fry - try

pancake - for goodness sake!

toast - boast

glass - at last!

Picking Up

busy - tizzy

mess - guess

clothes - pantyhose

book - look

box - socks

ball - hall

teddy bear - everywhere

Bath Time

time - grime

bath - math

soap - hope

bubble - trouble

towel - scowl

dry - cry

clean - dream

Getting Ready for Dinner

table - able

plate - date

spoon - cartoon

fork - pork or cork

mood - food

glasses - molasses

napkin - win

Helping Around the House

trash - smash

laundry - free

dishes - wishes

bed - said

sheet - beat

vacuum - room

dust - fussed

Grab Bag · · · · · · · · · · · · · · · ·

For these activities to be successful in stimulating interhemispheric transfers, remember several key elements. The student must use his left hand when feeling items. The student must verbalize what he feels and then must use descriptive language to defend that choice.

Level 1: Free-Choice Identification

Place a variety of objects into a bag. Direct the student to put his left hand into the bag, feel one item, and tell what it is. Then, have the student use descriptive words to support the identification of the object. Finally, the student pulls the object out of the bag to verify its identity. Replace the object into the bag before the student begins to identify the next object.

Level 2: Directed Identification

Place a variety of objects into a bag. Name one of the objects and ask the student to use her left hand to locate that object in the bag. Once the student isolates the target object, have her use descriptive language to tell how she knows it's the target object.

Level 3: Identification by Category

Gather six to eight items from a category, such as buttons. Objects that work well for this activity include beads, buttons, rocks, pens, combs, rubber bands, toothpicks, screws, dried pasta, or beans. Have at least three identical pairs from the category. Place all of these items into a bag, except for one item from each identical pair. Then, display these duplicate items in front of the student. Ask him to choose one of these items with his left hand and feel it to get a tactile imprint. Then, have the student reach into the bag with his left hand and find the item that matches the one he handled. Have the student use descriptive language to defend his choice.

Paper-and-Pencil Activities · · · · · · · · · ·

Paper-and-pencil activities help the student learn how to function within a multimodality environment and help prepare her for the note-taking activities that are an inevitable part of school. The student engages in activities requiring processing simple information and giving a fine-motor response, followed by a verbal response. The student will need paper, a pencil, and a box of crayons.

Set 1

1. Listen to these letters and write the second one. *C, F, E*
2. When I name an animal, write what it says. *Cow*
3. Listen to these numbers and write down the third one. *8, 4, 7, 1*

4. When I name a color, get the crayon that matches it and draw a circle. Black
5. Listen to these shapes and draw the second one. Circle, star, diamond
6. Listen to these letters and write down the fourth one. *M, N, L, S, T*
7. When I name an animal, write what is says. Chicken
8. Listen to these shapes and draw the fourth one. Star, diamond, square, circle, oval
9. Listen to these numbers and write down the fourth one. *2, 6, 5, 9, 3*
10. When I name a color, get the crayon that matches it and draw a circle. Purple

Set 2

1. Listen to these letters and write the first one. *A, B*
2. When I name an animal, write what it says. Pig
3. Listen to these shapes and draw the second one. Square, rectangle, triangle
4. Listen to these numbers and write the fifth one. *5, 3, 6, 4, 1, 2*
5. When I name a color, get the crayon that matches it and draw a circle. Green
6. Listen to these numbers and write the fourth one. *10, 12, 9, 7, 4*
7. When I name a color, get the crayon that matches it and draw a circle. Purple
8. Listen to these shapes and draw the third one. Oval, triangle, diamond, circle
9. When I name an animal, write what it says. Duck
10. Listen to these letters and write the third one. *Z, Y, W, X*

Set 3

1. Listen to these shapes and draw the first one. Square, circle
2. Listen to these letters and write the fifth one. *M, O, L, R, B, K*
3. When I name an animal, write what it says. Horse
4. When I name a color, find the crayon that matches it and draw a circle. Black
5. Listen to these numbers and write the third one. *3, 5, 4, 6*
6. When I name a color, get the crayon that matches and draw a circle. Red
7. Listen to these numbers and write the second one. *4, 7, 1*
8. Listen to these shapes and draw the third one. Rectangle, diamond, oval, square
9. Listen to these long vowels and write the fourth one. *E, A, I, O, U*
10. When I name an animal, write what it says. Sheep

Set 4

1. Listen to these shapes and draw the second one. Hexagon, pentagon, diamond, oval
2. When I name a color, get the crayon that matches it and draw a circle. Green
3. Listen to these numbers and write the third one. *4, 7, 2, 8*
4. Listen to these shapes and draw the first one. Oval, circle

5. When I name a color, get the crayon that matches it and draw a circle. Yellow
6. Listen to these letters and write the second one. *C, S, G*
7. When I name an animal, write what it says. Turkey
8. Listen to these letters and write the fourth one. *H, I, J, N, D*
9. When I name an animal, write what it says. Duck
10. Listen to these numbers and write the second one. *6, 9, 12*

Set 5

1. When I name an animal, write what it says. Rooster
2. Listen to these numbers and write the third one. *5, 10, 15, 20*
3. Listen to these shapes and draw the second one. Diamond, triangle, oval
4. When I name a color, get the crayon that matches it and draw a circle. Brown
5. Listen to these letters and write the third one. *A, C, K, R*
6. When I name a color, get the crayon that matches it and draw a circle. Orange
7. When I name an animal, write what it says. Donkey
8. Listen to these numbers and write the fourth one. *10, 9, 8, 7, 6*
9. Listen to these shapes and draw the third one. Oval, rectangle, square, circle
10. Listen to these letters and write the second one. *T, X, P*

Set 6

1. Listen to these numbers and write the second one. *5, 10, 8*
2. Listen to these shapes and draw the second one. Circle, square, triangle
3. Listen to these letters and write the third one. *L, V, D, G*
4. When I name an animal, write what it says. Frog
5. When I name a color, get the crayon that matches it and draw a circle. Blue
6. Listen to these numbers and write the fourth one. *1, 3, 11, 9, 13*
7. When I name a color, get the crayon that matches it and draw a circle. Red
8. When I name an animal, write what it says. Bird
9. Listen to these letters and write the first one. *Q, O*
10. Listen to these shapes and draw the first one. Triangle, oval

Singing to Scale . . . .

This activity requires using a xylophone. Hit a note on the xylophone and sing it for two seconds. Then, hand the mallet to the student. Direct him to hit any note on the xylophone and sing it, being sure to match his voice pitch with the actual note.

Drawing to Directions . . . .

Give the student oral directions for these riddles. Provide paper, a pencil, and a box of crayons. After the student writes or draws each response, ask an appropriate question so the student can verbalize his response.

Level 1: Target Identified

Tell the student you will name something common and the student will draw just the outline of what you have named. The drawing should be large enough to add details as you present them to make the drawing more specific. Present up to three of these drawings per training session.

1. Draw a house.
   a. Draw two large windows.
   b. Draw two small windows.
   c. Draw a brick chimney.
   d. Color the house yellow.
   e. Draw a doorbell to the right of the front door.

2. Draw a bike.
   a. Draw a basket on the handlebars.
   b. Draw pink streamers coming from both handlebars.
   c. Color the seat brown.
   d. Draw a fender over the back tire.
   e. Draw a red reflector on the back fender.

3. Draw a bed.
   a. Draw two pillows at the head of the bed.
   b. Draw a pillow at the foot of the bed.
   c. Color all the pillows orange.
   d. Draw a dust ruffle along the bottom of the bed.
   e. Make a striped pattern with your orange crayon on the dust ruffle.

4. Draw a wagon.
   a. Color the handle and tires black.
   b. Color the wagon red.
   c. Draw a red bow on the handle.
   d. Draw a small bird on the side of the wagon.
   e. Draw a small brown box in the wagon.

5. Draw a car.
   a. Make the car a convertible by coloring the top brown.
   b. Draw raindrops on the car.
   c. Color the car light gray.
   d. Draw an antenna on the front hood.
   e. Draw a small orange and blue flag on the antenna.

6. Draw a boat.
   a. Draw two portholes on the boat.
   b. Draw one large sail on the boat.
   c. Draw an apple on the sail.
   d. Color the sail blue.
   e. Draw a motor on the back of the boat.

7. Draw a bird.
   a. Draw a large, hooked beak.
   b. Color the beak yellow.
   c. Draw four red feathers for the bird's tail.
   d. Draw a small, brown worm hanging from the beak.
   e. Draw a stick in one claw.

8. Draw a dog.
   a. Draw a collar around its neck.
   b. Draw four black buttons on the collar.
   c. Color the collar red.
   d. Draw a black spot on the dog's head and one on its back.
   e. Color the dog light brown.

9. Draw a stove.
   a. Draw four burners on the stove.
   b. Draw a large pan on one burner.
   c. Draw a frying pan on another burner.
   d. Color the stove light gray.
   e. Outline the burners with your black crayon.

10. Draw a long-sleeved shirt.
    a. Draw a button-down collar on the shirt.
    b. Draw a pocket on each side of the shirt.
    c. Draw four black buttons going down the front of the shirt.
    d. Draw one black button on each pocket.
    e. Draw thin, black stripes on the shirt.

11. Draw an envelope.
    a. Write you first name in the upper-left corner.
    b. Write your last name in the middle of the envelope.
    c. Draw a stamp in the upper-right corner.
    d. Highlight your first name with the orange crayon.
    e. Highlight your last name with the yellow crayon.

12. Draw a swimming pool.
    a. Write the number *8* at one end.
    b. Write the number *3* at the other end.
    c. Draw a ladder with three steps going into the pool.
    d. Draw a yellow ring tube in the middle of the pool.
    e. Draw a diving board at the deep end of the pool.

13. Draw a desk.
    a. Draw a telephone on the right side of the desk.
    b. Draw a study lamp on the left side of the desk.
    c. Draw a pad of paper in the middle of the desk.
    d. Draw a pencil on top of the pad.
    e. Draw a stapler to the right of the pad.

14. Draw a bookcase.
    a. Draw four shelves in the bookcase.
    b. Draw three books on the bottom shelf.
    c. Draw a vase on the second shelf from the bottom.
    d. Draw a clock on the third shelf from the bottom.
    e. Draw a pile of magazines on the top shelf.

15. Draw a picture frame.
    a. Draw sand at the bottom of the picture.
    b. Draw some sea grass growing out of the sand.
    c. Draw a fish in the middle of the picture.
    d. Draw three bubbles coming out of the fish's mouth.
    e. Draw a starfish to the left of the fish.

16. Draw a table.
    a. Draw three chairs around the table.
    b. Draw a plate and a glass in front of each chair.
    c. Draw a napkin folded in half to the left of each plate.
    d. Draw a fork on top of each napkin.
    e. Draw a cake in the middle of the table.

17. Draw a large pumpkin.
    a. Draw a stem at the top.
    b. Draw a small, black triangle in the middle.
    c. Draw a small, red circle for the eye on the right.
    d. Draw a small, blue square for the eye on the left.
    e. Draw a large, green mouth.

18. Draw a Mrs. Potato Head®.
    a. Draw a yellow earring on each ear.
    b. Show her wearing a pair of green glasses.
    c. Draw her tongue sticking out.
    d. Draw a yellow cap on her head.
    e. Draw a red purse on her arm.

Level 2: Target Unidentified

Tell the student you will present a series of directions the student should follow to create a picture. When you have finished giving the directions, ask the student, "What did you draw?" After he answers, have him describe the picture. Answers are provided in parentheses at the end of the directions for each picture.

1. a. Draw an orange circle.
   b. Draw four curved, vertical lines on the circle.
   c. Draw a triangle in the middle of the circle.
   d. Draw a small, brown square at the top of the circle.
   e. Draw two upside-down triangles in the upper part of the circle. (jack-o'-lantern)

2. a. Draw three small circles, one on top of the other.
   b. Draw a small, black square on top of the top circle.
   c. Draw two eyes on the top circle.
   d. Draw a black button in the middle of the second and third circles.
   e. Draw a broom on either side of the circles. (snowman)

3. a. Draw five small circles, side by side.
   b. Write the letter *V* on top of the first circle.
   c. Draw two eyes on the first circle.
   d. Draw a small triangle under each circle.
   e. Draw small lines around the circles to make them look fuzzy. (caterpillar)

4. a. Draw a rectangle.
   b. Draw a small circle under each bottom corner of the rectangle.
   c. Draw a small square on top of the rectangle, in the middle.
   d. Draw a small circle on the left side of the square.
   e. Draw smoke coming from the lower-right side of the rectangle. (car)

5. a. Draw a rectangle.
   b. Draw two small circles under each bottom corner of the rectangle.
   c. Draw a small square coming off the upper-left corner of the rectangle.
   d. Draw a bigger square coming off the upper-right corner of the rectangle.
   e. Draw smoke coming from the big square. (train)

6. a. Draw a rectangle.
   b. Draw a small circle under each bottom corner of the rectangle.
   c. Draw a short, horizontal line coming from the right side of the rectangle.
   d. Draw a small square at the end of that line.
   e. Color the rectangle red. (wagon)

7. a. Draw a rectangle.
   b. In the left side of the rectangle, write the letters *MJK*.
   c. In the right side of the rectangle, write the numbers *318*.
   d. Draw a small square in the upper-right corner.
   e. Color the rectangle light blue. (license plate)

8. a. Draw an upside-down pear shape.
   b. Draw polka dots on the pear shape
   c. Draw two vertical lines coming from each bottom side of the pear shape.
   d. Draw a square at the end of the lines.
   e. Color the square brown. (hot-air balloon)

9. a. Draw a horizontal rectangle.
   b. Draw four small, vertical rectangles in a row across the middle.
   c. Draw a small circle above and below each rectangle.
   d. Draw a line through the middle of each circle.
   e. Color everything white. (light switches)

10. a. Draw a circle.
    b. Draw a dot in the middle of the circle.
    c. Draw a short arrow pointing away from the dot in any direction.
    d. Draw a longer arrow pointing away from the dot in any direction.
    e. Write the number *12* at the top of the circle. (clock)

11. a. Draw a tall rectangle.
    b. Draw four rows of three small circles each in the rectangle.
    c. Draw a tic-tac-toe grid in the bottom circle on the right side.
    d. Draw an *X* with a small, horizontal line through it in the bottom circle on the left side.
    e. Write the number *0* in the bottom circle in the middle. (cordless phone)

12. a. Draw a small triangle.
    b. Draw a larger triangle below that first triangle.
    c. Draw a still larger triangle below that second triangle.
    d. Draw a small square under the middle part of the largest triangle.
    e. Color the triangles green. (pine tree)

13. a. Draw two vertical lines about one inch apart.
    b. Connect the vertical lines with three evenly-spaced, horizontal lines.
    c. Draw a curved line sloping down from the vertical line on the right side.
    d. Draw a stick figure of a boy standing on the top horizontal line.
    e. Draw another boy standing next to the end of the curved line. (slide)

14. a. Draw a large square.
    b. Draw two vertical lines about an inch apart, from the top to the bottom of the square.
    c. Connect the vertical lines with five horizontal lines, evenly spaced.
    d. Draw a boy standing at the top of the square and between the vertical lines.
    e. Draw some grass at the bottom of the square. (boy standing on a wall)

15. a. Draw a vertical line about two inches long.
    b. Draw a small box touching the right side of the line just below the middle.
    c. Cover the box with diagonal lines.
    d. Draw a short, vertical line from the bottom-right corner of the box.
    e. Draw a short, horizontal line to connect the two vertical lines. (chair)

16. a. Draw two circles, about an inch apart. Connect them with a horizontal line.
    b. Draw a short, vertical line rising from the right side of the horizontal line.
    c. Write the letter *U* sideways across the top of the vertical line. Be sure that the opening is facing toward the left.
    d. Draw a short, vertical line rising from the left side of the horizontal line.
    e. Draw an oval on top of this vertical line. (bike)

17. a. Draw the bottom half of an oval.
    b. Draw a horizontal line across the top of the oval.
    c. Draw two small circles in the oval.
    d. Draw a vertical line rising from the middle of the oval.
    e. Attach the letter *V* to the vertical line to form a triangle. (sailboat)

18. a. Draw the top half of an oval.
    b. Draw another oval underneath the first oval. Be sure to make it longer on each side than the first oval.
    c. Draw the bottom half of an oval underneath the second oval.
    d. Color the middle oval brown.
    e. Draw a thin, red line on top on the brown oval. (hamburger with ketchup)

Opposites . . . .

In this activity, the student listens to simple information and gives a gross- or fine-motor response incorporating the element of processing antonyms to increase the level of difficulty. After giving the motor response, the student is instructed to defend his answer when you ask, "Why did you do that?" Accept answers that differ from your expectations as long as the student defends his response with good logic.

Tell the student, "I'll give you a direction. Then, I want you to do the opposite of what I told you to do."

Set 1
materials: assorted crayons, including a white and a black crayon
1. Hop on your right foot.
2. Look up.
3. Take two steps forward.
4. Stand in front of the table.
5. Walk to the door.
6. Stamp your feet loudly.
7. Snap your fingers quickly.
8. Make a happy face.
9. Get a white crayon.
10. Raise your hands high.

Set 2
materials: white paper, black paper, chair
1. Walk toward the door.
2. Click your tongue softly.
3. Stand in back of the chair.
4. Make a sad face.
5. Run around the table.
6. Say "She sells sea shells" slowly.
7. Get a piece of black paper.
8. Stand on your left foot.
9. Crouch down low.
10. Sit down.

Set 3

materials: ball, pictures of a white and a black snowman, scissors

1. Walk into the hallway.
2. Laugh as though you're very happy.
3. Hold up all of your fingers.
4. Touch your right ear.
5. Say "Peter Piper Peter Pumpkin" quickly.
6. Cut out the black snowman.
7. Take three steps backward.
8. Clap your hands loudly.
9. Throw a ball up high.
10. Stand in front of the desk.

Set 4

materials: paper clips, pictures (1 boy, 1 girl), blocks, book, pencil, paper

1. Put this paper clip in your right hand.
2. Point to a picture of a boy.
3. Show me two things in this room that are the same color.
4. Build a tower using an even number of blocks.
5. Put a book on the table.
6. Add *5* and *3*. Then, tell me your answer.
7. Hold a pencil below the table.
8. Open a book to the first page.
9. Pick up something that is soft.
10. Draw a picture of a cup and a plate and draw the plate first.

Set 5

materials: blocks, paper, crayons, chalk and chalkboard, pencil, paper clips

1. Build a tower using an odd number of blocks.
2. Subtract *3* from *5*. Then, use blocks to show your answer.
3. Blink your eyes quickly.
4. Draw a picture of something that is soft.
5. Write a girl's name on a piece of paper.
6. Hold up two colors that begin with different letters.
7. Draw a long line on the chalkboard.
8. Stand to the left of your chair.
9. Put the pencil and paper clip in your pocket and put the pencil in last.
10. Hold a piece of paper above the table.

Set 6

materials: raisins, pencils, crayons, paper, various sizes of paper clips

1. Pick up a dark-colored crayon.
2. Bang the table with something that is hard.
3. Stand up and say your name.
4. On a piece of paper, draw half a cookie.
5. Draw a short line on the paper.
6. Put your feet on the table.
7. Close your mouth tightly.
8. Write a boy's name on the paper.
9. Draw a whole cookie.
10. Pick up a small paper clip.

In addition to providing quality therapy for the student presenting with central auditory processing deficits (CAPD), provide other compensatory strategies and environmental management options to help the student obtain maximum, positive changes. Everyone involved in both school and home environments should work together to achieve the maximum consistency of change.

Compensatory Strategies

Involve the student, yourself, key teachers, and the student's parents or caregivers in reviewing the list of strategies below. Instruct the student to assume responsibility to use these strategies as needed. Instruct the teachers and parents or caregivers that their familiarity with the strategies will help the student to manage CAPD difficulties more effectively.

- Obtain the student's attention before presenting auditory information. Some of the following techniques may be helpful:

   Give a verbal cue to get the student's attention, such as these:
   "Listen."   "It's my turn to talk."
   "Get ready."   Say the student's name.

   Talk with the student to agree on a physical cue to signal for attention, such as tapping the student's desk or touching the student lightly on the shoulder.

- Require appropriate eye contact from the student. Remind the student of the importance of eye contact by ceasing talking whenever the student looks away.

- Encourage students who have difficulty with background noise to wear ear plugs while working individually within the classroom. When instructing or giving directions, encourage the student to use listening devices as appropriate.

- Teachers, clinicians, and parents should speak slowly and clearly; use simple, brief language for directions; and give directions in a logical progression. Words that add clarity to sequence, such as first, next, and finally are crucial to help the student understand directions readily.

- Information presented to the student should incorporate repeating, rephrasing, and paraphrasing the content of the presentation. Examples, illustrations, demonstrations, visual aids, written instructions, and gestures are all excellent supplements.

- Present directions and new information in small units during several short sessions, incorporating breaks between tasks. Allow for one task to be completed prior to presenting information pertaining to the next task.

- Before introducing new content, give pre-instructions with emphasis on main ideas and key words presented at both auditory and visual levels. Provide the student with pre-written notes, encourage the use of a tape recorder during lectures, and assign a buddy to take notes so that the student can devote full visual attention to supplement the auditory channel. Avoid note-taking activities (simultaneous listening and writing activities) as much as possible.

- When speaking to the student, vary your vocal intensity and pitch levels to maintain maximum attention.

- When giving directions, pause briefly at logical points of completion to allow the student additional processing time. For example: "Go into the pantry. (Pause.) Look on the second shelf. (Pause.) Bring me the can of tomatoes."

- To ensure that the student listens for meaning rather than for repeating what you say, require ongoing feedback from her as you present information. Ask questions, answer the student's questions, and summarize what you've said periodically.

- Students with CAPD require more time to process directions, questions, and conversations. Give the student the "gift of time" to process before expecting a response.

- Instruct the student that taking personal responsibility and playing an active role in managing any identified weaknesses will result in success at home and school.

- Here are some things the student can do to take responsibility:

    Check all work carefully.

    Maintain consistent organization in every aspect of daily life.

    Ask for additional information and clarification of presented material as needed.

    Analyze and restructure tasks and directions into smaller, simpler units to execute carefully.

Environmental Management . . . .

The student, clinician, teachers, and parents or caregivers should review the ways to manage the environment, listed below. Everyone involved must cooperate about management issues in order to help the student manage CAPD factors effectively.

- Seat the student close to the instructor. Allow for flexibility in the room. When the teacher moves toward the chalkboard, the student should be able to shift seating accordingly.

- Minimize auditory distractions for the student. Seat the student away from open windows or doors, computers and printers, bathrooms, and pencil sharpeners.

- Minimize visual distractions for the student. Face the student's desk away from the windows. Seating the student in the front of the room will also minimize visual distractions of classmates seated behind the student or moving around the room.

- Avoid open classroom seating for the student and be sensitive to areas with reverberating sound in considering classroom placement alternatives.

- Reinforce a positive, nurturing environment for the student. Here are some specific techniques:

    Avoid showing frustration when the student misunderstands information.

    Praise even the small successes and minimal improvements.

    Give frequent feedback about how well the student is managing and compensating within areas of weakness as well as the strengths you observe. Communicate with the team involved in supporting the student, too, to keep everyone informed.

    Be responsive to the student's questions and requests for assistance.

- Structure home, school, and therapy environments to promote as much consistency as possible. This consistency boosts the student's ability to predict what's expected in various routines and formats. Encourage the student to wear a watch, use assignment books, and use calendars to adhere to clearly-defined routines.

- Provide for redundancy within the classroom environment. Material needs to be rephrased and represented in alternative forms, such as adding visuals or incorporating hands-on experiences. Additionally, pre-teach material and give the student pre-written notes to follow. To build in extra teaching redundancy, have teachers tape record their lectures and allow the student to use a classmate's notes as a review.

- Watch the student closely to ensure adequate comprehension. Just because a student can repeat directions verbatim does not necessarily mean the student understands those directions. Here are some ways to check the student's understanding of directions or instructions:

    Watch the student follow the direction.

    As you present instructions, have the student paraphrase the information prior to beginning the task.

    Have the student demonstrate what to do, based on your instructions, before beginning the task.

- Educate involved teachers that the student will continue to have great difficulty within the classroom without their support and cooperation. Help the teachers accept the premise that all children in the class need to learn the targeted material. Successful teachers will ensure that each student learns that material in a manner best suited to the individual child, be it through the use of visual aids, auditory aids, or whatever is required to meet the student's unique needs.

Bellis, Teri James. *Assessment and Management of Central Auditory Processing Disorders in the Educational Setting.* San Diego, CA: Singular Publishing Group, Inc., 1996.

Chermak, Gail D., and Musiek, Frank E. *Central Auditory Processing Disorders: New Perspectives.* San Diego, CA: Singular Publishing Group, Inc., 1997.

Ferre, Jeanane M. *Processing Power: A Guide to CAPD Assessment and Treatment.* San Antonio, TX: The Psychological Corporation, 1997.

Gillet, Pamela. *Auditory Processes.* Novato, CA: Academic Therapy Publications, 1993.

Hamaguchi, Patricia McAleer. *It's Time to Listen: A Program for Children with Listening Problems.* San Antonio, TX: The Psychological Corporation, 1995.

Kelly, Dorothy. *Thera Guides: Understanding Central Auditory Processing Disorder.* San Antonio, TX: The Psychological Corporation, 1998.

Kelly, Dorothy A. *Central Auditory Processing Disorder: Strategies for Use with Children and Adolescents.* San Antonio, TX: The Psychological Corporation, 1995.

Masters, M. Gay, Steeker, Nancy A., and Katz, Jack. *Central Auditory Processing.* Des Moines, IA: Allyn & Bacon, 1998.

Sollier, Pierre. "Overview of the Tomatis AE Method," 1996. [Online]. Available: http://www. tomatis.com/overview.html/.

19-06-9